HEART TALKS

A Volume of Confidential Talks
on the Problems, Privileges, and
Duties of the Christian Life, Designed to Comfort, Encourage,
Strengthen and Instruct

By C. W. NAYLOR

GOSPEL TRUMPET COMPANY
Anderson, Indiana,   -   -   U. S. A.

Heart Talks
By Charles W. Naylor

© 1922 Gospel Trumpet Company
© 2007 Reformation Publishers

Printed On Demand 2007

Trade Paper
ISBN 978-1-60416-091-8   Item #00281

Trade Cloth
ISBN 978-1-60416-092-5   Item #01917

Reformation Publishers
242 University Drive
Prestonsburg KY 41653
606-886-7224
Fax 606-886-8222
rpublisher@aol.com

Printed and bound in the United States of America

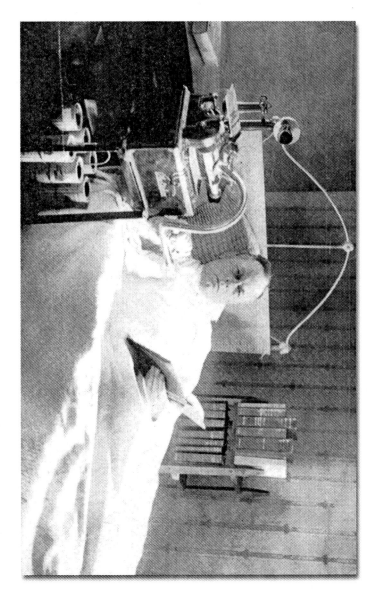

C. W. NAYLOR

SEE PAGE V

CONCERNING THE AUTHOR

The author of ''Heart Talks'' has been peculiarly qualified for his task by a training of the soul in the school of suffering. After thirteen years in the ministry, as a result of an internal injury he has been compelled to spend the last thirteen years in his bed day and night, a constant sufferer. He has known the experience of long and intense suffering with no hope of relief from any human source, and with no other prospect for the future than that of remaining a helpless invalid for life and without a means of earning a livelihood. He has learned the lesson of patience through suffering. He has learned to trust God for the supply of his temporal needs because there was no other to trust. He has learned to commune with God by being deprived of the opportunity of mingling much with his fellow men.

Yet he has not lost the joy out of life. He still does what he can to build up the kingdom of God and bless his fellow men by his words of good cheer. He is still interested in the events of the world, and especially in the progress of God's work. He has demonstrated the efficacy of God's grace to sustain one and give joy in the very discouraging circumstances of life. Though a firm believer in divine healing, and instrumental in the healing of those who kneel at his bedside for prayer, yet he has not received permanent healing, because, as he believes, this is God's method of developing his heart and making him more useful in helping others.

During the last five years especially he has contributed regularly to a religious periodical articles on subjects similar to those in this book, besides conducting a ''Questions Answered'' and information department, and writing a number of books.

The Publishers.

PREFACE

Most of the miscellaneous writings of which this volume is composed appeared originally in serial form. The widespread interest produced by them, the hundreds of letters of appreciation, and the numerous earnest requests for their publication in permanent form have been the moving cause for their presentation in this volume. They cover a very wide range of topics, are written in a popular style, and deal with phases of life and personal experience that are all too much neglected but which every Christian needs to understand. Each paper is complete in itself, though all have a general relation. They are pastoral in nature and have by the blessings of God comforted, encouraged, strengthened, and enlightened many souls. That they may by divine help continue to be a blessing to many is the earnest desire of

THE AUTHOR.

Anderson, Ind., May 14, 1920.

CONTENTS

HEART TALKS

TALK ONE

WHAT IT MEANS TO TRUST THE LORD

Throughout the Bible we are exhorted again and again to trust in the Lord. We are warned against trusting in princes, in riches, or in ourselves; for all such trust is vain. Trusting in the Lord is represented as being safe, as blessed, and as producing very desirable results. In it is our hope, our strength, our safety, and our help.

But what does trust mean? It does not mean carelessness or indifference. Just to let things go and say, "Oh, I guess it will come out all right," is not trusting. Just drifting heedlessly with the tide is not trust. Neglect is not trust. Trust is something positive. It is a real something, not a mere happen-so or maybe-so. It is a definite attitude of soul and mind, a realization of our own need and of God's sufficiency. It is the reaching out and anchoring of ourselves in God.

The soul who really trusts is not driven about by every wind. The waves beat against him as they beat against the anchored ship, but they can not dash him upon the rocks; for he who trusts in God is strong, because he has the strength of God.

Trust does not mean shutting our eyes to facts. There is no such thing as "blind faith." Trust looks at things as they are. It sees the dangers that threaten, and

xi

assesses them at their true value. It sees the need, and
does not try to disguise it. It sees the difficulties, and
does not discount them. But seeing all this, it looks
beyond and sees God, its all-sufficient help. It sees him
greater than the needs or the dangers or the difficulties,
and it does not shrink before them.

There is no fear in trust: the two are opposites. When
we really fear, we are not fully trusting. When we trust,
fear gives way to assurance. Fear is tormenting. How
many there are who are constantly agitated by fear!
They fear the devil, trials, temptations, the wind, lightning, burglars, and a thousand other things. Their
days are haunted by fear of this thing or that. Their
peace is marred and their hearts are troubled. For all
this, trust is the cure. I do not mean to say that if you
trust, nothing will ever startle you or frighten you, or
that you will never feel physical fear in time of danger;
but in such times trust will bring to us a consciousness
that the Lord knows and cares, and that his helping
presence is with us.

When John Wesley was crossing the Atlantic from
England to America to become a missionary to the
Indians, the ship on which he was sailing encountered
a terrible storm. It seemed that those on board would
be lost. Many were much alarmed and were in deep
distress. Wesley himself was one of this number. In
the midst of the storm his attention was attracted to
some Moravians who sat calm and undisturbed by the
dangers about them. Wesley greatly wondered at their
untroubled appearance. He inquired why it was. Their
reply was that they were trusting in the Lord and that

they had in their souls the consciousness of his protecting presence and care. They felt no fear because there was nothing threatening that a Christian had need to fear. Mr. Wesley did not have such an experience, but what he learned from those simple-hearted people caused him to seek a similar experience.

There is no worry in trust. When we worry about anything, we have not committed it to God. Trust takes away the anxiety. So many people use up a large portion of their energy in worry. There is always something troubling them. Their days and nights are full of anxiety. Worrying becomes a fixed habit with them. Peace and calmness and assurance find but little room in their lives. The cure for all this is trust. Trust brings confidence. Trust whispers to our souls that there is no cause to worry. It tells us that God holds the helm of our vessel. It bids us to be of good courage, assuring us that God is our refuge and strength, that our lives and all are in his hands, and that he will work out for us the things that are best.

O soul, stop worrying, and trust. It is so much better. If you find yourself worrying, stop right there Take your eyes off the things that trouble you; look up, and keep looking up till you see God and his infinite care for you. Remember that when you worry you are not trusting, and that when you trust you are not worrying. Worry depresses, discourages, and weakens. It never helps us in any way. It is always a hindrance to us. God wants to bring into our lives a peaceful calm like that of a summer evening. He would have us without anxiety, as care-free as the birds or the lilies. It is trust that brings us this experience. Will you not learn to trust? "Casting all your care on him; for he careth for you."

There is no murmuring in trust. When all is trusted into God's hands, it brings to us a feeling of satisfaction concerning God's dealings with us. We can sing from our hearts, "God's way is best; I will not murmur." When we trust, it is easy to praise. When we trust, the heart is full of thankful appreciation. If you are inclined to murmur, it is because you do not trust.

There is no feeling of bitterness when things do not go as we think they should, if we are trusting. Bitterness comes from rebellion, and there is no rebellion in trust. Trust can always say, "Not my will, but thine, be done."

In trust there is peace, the peace of God which passeth understanding. There is calm in the soul of him who trusts. There is no doubt in trust, for doubt is swallowed up in assurance, and assurance brings calmness and peace.

Trusting brings confidence. It permits us to see God in his true character. It causes us to realize the greatness and tenderness of his love. It gives us a consciousness of his might, and through it we are sheltered under his wings. By it our enemies lose their power; our dangers, their terrors. We have a consciousness of safety, and that brings rest. He has said, "Ye shall find rest unto your souls." He who trusts finds this soul-rest. God has not given us turmoil and trouble. He has said, "In me ye shall have peace"; and again, "My peace I give unto you." Are not these precious promises?

Are they true in your life? God means that they shall be. Trust will make them real to you. They never can be real until you learn to trust. Trust is the root that upholds and nourishes the tree of Christian life. It is trust that causes it to blossom and to bring forth fruit, and the more fully you trust, the greater and richer and more profuse will be the fruits of your righteousness.

I have told you something about trust, but I now wish to speak of some other things that belong to trust. Trust implies submission. Very often God fails to do things for us because we do not permit him to. We want to plan for ourselves. We want things to be done in the way that seems best to our finite wisdom.

Too many of us are like a woman whose husband recently said that they had often gone driving together, that their horse would sometimes become frightened, and that when it did, his wife would also become frightened and would almost invariably seize the lines. Thus, he would have to manage both his wife and the horse, making his task doubly difficult.

How many of us are just like that woman! When anything threatens, we become alarmed and try to help God. We feel that it is not safe to leave all in his hands and let him manage the circumstances. Our failure to submit to him often complicates matters, and it is harder for him to manage us than it is to manage the difficulties. To trust God means to keep our hands off the lines. It means to let him have his way and do things as he thinks best. It may be a hard lesson to learn, but you will hinder God until you learn it.

"It is God which worketh in you both to will and to

do of his good pleasure" (Phil. 2:13). If your life is submitted to him, he will work in you to will as well as to do. He will help do the planning as well as the working out. He will aid you in the choosing, no less than in the doing. If you can not submit to him thus, you have not reached the place where you can trust. You must first learn to take your hands off yourself and off circumstances; then trust will be natural and easy. How can you trust him if you are not willing for him to do just as it pleases him? When you have submitted all and he has his way fully with you, then the blessed fruitfulness of trust will come into your life.

Trust also implies obedience. It means working with God to produce the results. We can not sit down and fold our hands in idleness and expect things to work themselves out. We must be workers, not shirkers. The man who prays for a bountiful harvest but prepares no ground and plants no seed will pray in vain. Faith and works must go together. We must permit God to *direct* our efforts and *command* our efforts. We must be willing to work when he wants us to work and in the way he wants us to work. Our attempts to trust will amount to nothing if we are not willing to obey. Right here is the secret of many people's trouble; they are willing to obey so long as the thing commanded is what they themselves would choose, but when it is otherwise they are not so ready. Our obedience must be full and willing, or we can not trust.

Trust implies patience. Even God can not work everything out immediately. We are told that "ye have need of patience, that, after ye have done the will of

God, ye might receive the promise" (Heb. 10:36). So many times we want the answers to our prayers right away. If they do not come thus, we grow impatient and think God is not going to answer. There is no use trying to hurry the Lord; we shall only hinder him if we do. He will not work according to our plans, but according to his own. Time does not matter so much to the eternal One as it does to us.

A brother once came to the altar in a meeting I helped to hold. In telling his trouble he said, "When I want anything done, it has to be done in a hurry." Many other people can not be patient and wait. They want it *now*. This is a great hindrance to their faith. The Psalmist says, "Rest in the Lord, and wait patiently for him" (Psa. 37:7). We are not only to wait patiently for him to work out his purpose, but we are at the same time to *rest* in him. Some people can wait, but they can not rest at the same time. They are uneasy and impatient; they want to hurry the Lord all the time. The result usually is that their faith does not last very long. You must add patience to your faith to make it effective. If you really trust, you can be patient. It may not aways be easy, but the more perfect your trust, the easier it will be to be patient.

When Luther was summoned to meet the diet for trial on a charge of heresy, his friends, fearing for his life, tried to persuade him not to go; but he declared that he would go even if there were as many devils there as there were tiles on the housetops. He trusted God, and that trust gave him an unwavering courage. Three Hebrews trusted God, and the fiery furnace could not even singe their garments. Daniel trusted God, and the hungry lions could not touch him. Many thousands of others have trusted God with similar results.

But trusting God is an active, positive thing. A passive submission or surrender to circumstances is not trust. Trusting the Lord to save us means to definitely rely on him to do it; to confidently expect that he will do it. This leads directly to the confident trust that he does do it. It brings the conscious assurance that it is an accomplished fact. We are not left to doubt, to hope, or to guess; but we have a positive trust that brings a positive result.

The same is true of sanctification. A positive faith brings a positive experience; and so long as our faith remains positive, the experience remains positive. It is only when faith begins to waver and doubts appear that the experience becomes uncertain. If you will maintain a positive faith, God will take care of your experience. Here lies the secret of continuous victory. There may be conflicts, but faith is the foundation of sure victory.

Trusting the Lord for healing means more than refusing to employ a physician and to take drugs. People who do not trust God at all often refuse to use drugs. They may at no time during their sickness really exercise an act of faith for healing. They simply surrender to existing conditions and hope that it will come out all right. In many such cases nature will overcome the disease, and the person will recover. The "prayer of faith," however, is positive; it saves the sick; it brings healing. Sometimes the sick person, because of the mental effects of his sickness, is not able to exercise faith;

but when he is able, faith will be an active, positive thing with him, if the desired results are to follow.

It is safe to trust in the Lord. Isaiah says, "I will trust, and not be afraid" (Isa. 12:2). That is the way God wants us to trust. He would have us be confident in him. But sometimes we get to looking at circumstances, and they loom up so threateningly before us that in spite of ourselves we tremble and shrink before them. We believe that God will take care of us and help us, but we can not quiet our fears. Our feelings are very much as they are when we stand just outside the bars of the cage of a ferocious wild beast. We know it can not reach us; we know we are safe from those powerful teeth and claws; but still we can not help having a feeling that we should not have were we somewhere else. When he comes to our side of the cage, we shrink involuntarily, but still we trust the iron bars and do not run away.

The Psalmist tells us what to do when we have such fears. "What time I am afraid, I will trust in thee" (Psa. 56:3). Still keep trusting. God will not chide you for the fears you can not help, but only for those that come from unbelief. Trust in God. It is the safest thing you have ever done; and he will never fail you.

TALK TWO

THE BLESSING OF DISSATISFACTION

A young sister sat in a room one beautiful summer afternoon. The sound of the birds chirping on the lawn and other noises of the out-of-doors came in through the open window to her. There was a look of melancholy upon her face, and her gaze rested steadily upon the floor. It was clear that she was troubled about something. Just then a minister entered the room. Noticing her forlorn appearance, he said cheerily, "What is the matter, sister?"

She looked up at him and answered wearily, "O Brother A, I am so dissatisfied."

"Well," he replied, "I am glad of it."

She almost gasped with astonishment, and exclaimed, "Why, Brother A! what do you mean?"

He then sat down in a chair near her and explained to her the substance of what I am going to say to you.

We have all thought how good it is to be satisfied. How many times we have heard people testify and rejoice that they had reached this experience! I would not depreciate this sense of satisfaction, for out of it come many enjoyable things. It is a very pleasurable feeling and one that most people very earnestly desire. There are times, however, when such a feeling would be anything but a blessing. Perhaps this surprizes you as it did the sister. God has made provision to satisfy us. Christ said that he who would drink of the water of life should thirst no more; for it should be in him a well of water, and thus his thirst should be continually quenched. So there is a continual satisfaction in God. It is a good thing to be thus satisfied with God and his plans and ways and with our salvation, and dissatisfaction with any of these, if we are saved, is an evil to which we should not give place; but hardly any greater evil could come upon us than a complete and constant sense of satisfaction relating to our attainments in grace, the development of our spiritual powers, or the measures of our service to God.

Dissatisfaction is the mother of progress. The Chinese for centuries have been taught to be satisfied with having things like their fathers had. As a consequence they have almost entirely lost the inventive faculty. Long ago they were an inventive nation, but now an invention among them is a rarity. As long as people are satisfied, they are content to remain as they are. Satisfaction is the foe to progress. As long as you are fully satisfied, you are like a sailing-vessel in a dead calm. The sea about you may be very smooth. Everything may be very peaceful and serene. But all the time this calm prevails you are getting nowhere; you are at a standstill. It is only when the wind rises and the swells begin to move the vessel up and down and the sails begin to strain that good progress begins. You may feel very comfortable in your satisfaction. It may be very delightful and dreamy, but it may be dangerous also. Those who are fully satisfied for very long may be sure that there is need for an investigation. It is only when we become dissatisfied with present conditions and attainments that we are spurred to effectual effort to make progress.

Suppose God had been satisfied with world-conditions before Christ came. We should now have no Savior and no salvation. He was dissatisfied, thoroughly dissatisfied, and so he made the greatest sacrifice that he could make to change existing conditions. Paul was once very well satisfied with his place in the Jewish religion; he was not looking for anything better. His dissatisfaction arose from the fact that some other people were not satisfied thus but were finding and advocating something different. This aroused his severest condemnation. What he had was good enough for him and ought to be good enough for them.

There are many today who are just like Paul was. They are fully contented in their present situation, and should any one try to show them its insufficiency and the need of higher attainment, it would only arouse their opposition and indignation. That is why so many people oppose holiness. Just as soon as Paul saw Christ and the higher and better things for which Christ stood, he suddenly lost his satisfaction and became an earnest seeker for those better things. Sometimes it takes a rude shock to break through our self-satisfaction and to show us our true needs; but when it comes and arouses a dissatisfaction, it is truly a blessing.

Suppose Luther had been satisfied to continue in the Romish church, approving and submitting to her teachings and practises. Where might the world have been today? He became dissatisfied and gave voice to that dissatisfaction. Others heard and became dissatisfied. This dissatisfaction made their hearts hungry for God, and out of that heart-hunger came the Reformation.

Dissatisfaction has brought to us the multitude of new things which we have to use and enjoy. It has been because men became dissatisfied with old methods and old implements and old ideas and customs and old attainments that they have toiled in painful research, that they have labored night and day to invent new things. In some places people still plow with a crooked stick and grind their flour in hand-mills. What their fathers had is good enough for them. Some people are like that about religion. What their fathers had is good enough for them, and they are indignant if we even suggest something better; they are satisfied. There are others who sought and obtained a real experience of forgiveness, but right there they stopped. Years have passed. They were satisfied when they were first saved (which was a very good thing); the only trouble was that they remained satisfied and never made any further progress. They hear entire sanctification preached, they accept the doctrine intellectually, but they can never be persuaded to press on into the experience themselves. They go on from year to year and never make any real spiritual advancement. What is the trouble? Oh, they are just satisfied, that is all; and they will never get any further till their sleepy satisfaction is rudely broken in upon by something that startles them out of their security and awakens them to their needs. That will bring dissatisfaction and that in time will set them to seeking to have those needs supplied.

Some people are content just to drift with the tides. They go along with the crowd, whichever way sentiment goes, and are quite content. They are no real moral force in their community or in the church. They are aware of the fact, and they seem to be satisfied to have it so. They will never amount to very much so long as they are thus satisfied. Getting dissatisfied is the only thing that will ever make anything worth while of them.

There are those who know that they are less spiritual than they used to be; still, they are not much concerned about it. They are resting very easy. Such satisfaction is a curse. What such folks need is a good case of dissatisfaction; for that is the only thing that will keep them from drying up and withering away. I know of people who once had a glorious experience but who for years have been so satisfied with themselves that they have not progressed an inch. Instead, they have gone backwards, with the result that today they are cold and formal. They are still satisfied, they still profess to be justified and sanctified, but they amount to practically nothing for God or the church. There is no moral force radiating from their lives. To such persons the coming of dissatisfaction would be a great blessing. So long as they are satisfied with their present condition, so long they will be cold formalists.

Some people know that they are coming short both of their duty and of their privileges in the Lord, but in spite of this they seem content and are making no effort —at least no effective effort—to do better. O brother, sister, if you are satisfied where you ought to be dissatisfied, it is time you awakened, it is time you looked toward better things until your hunger for them stirred you to action to obtain them.

To those who are dissatisfied, who realize your needs

and lacks, I say: Do not be discouraged. God means by this very feeling of dissatisfaction with yourself to spur you on to seek diligently for higher and better attainments. If you allow yourself to be discouraged, it will only hinder you. God will help you to obtain that which you need. Do not falter because your need seems great; God's supply is more abundant than your need. Cast off every weight. Press forward. God will help you. When once he has aroused you to effort, you will find him ready to help. Your dissatisfaction is most encouraging. Do not stay dissatisfied; press on till you obtain what you need. You will never attain your full measure of desire in this life, but you may obtain much, and what you do obtain will prepare you for that fulness and satisfaction which only eternity can bring you.

Dissatisfaction is never welcome, but it is a true friend. Through it you may reach blessed attainments and soul-enriching grace. Value it and use it rightly, and it will prove a great blessing, though it may often be a blessing in disguise.

TALK THREE

WHY I BELIEVE THE OLD BOOK

Do I believe the old Book? Do I really believe it? My heart answers that I do. The deepest consciousness of my soul testifies that it is true. I will tell you some of the reasons why I believe it.

The Oldest, and Still the Newest, of Books

God's book written in the rocks is old, exceedingly old, but God's book the Bible reaches back still farther. It goes back not only to the "beginning" of this terrestrial world, but into eternity; for the expression, "in the beginning," used by John, reaches back long before this world was. "In the beginning was the Word, and the Word was with God, and the Word was God." From past eternity its majestic sweep covers the whole range of being and reaches into the future eternity. It is, in fact, the book of eternity, and within its folds lie the grandeur and sublimity of the great unknown future. It never gets out-of-date. Other books have their run of popularity and are forgotten, but the Bible never grows old; no matter how familiar we become with it, it is ever new. To the Christian it never grows stale, but is always fresh and always satisfying. It ever reveals new depths that we fail to fathom, new heights that we can not scale, and new beauties that enrapture our vision.

We read it over and over, and ever and anon we see new jewels sparkling within its pages, jewels that delight the eye and reflect the light of God. From it refreshing waters break out where we least expect them, and our souls are refreshed like a thirsty man who suddenly finds water on the desert. We may have read a text a thousand times, yet when we look at it again it opens up and presents to us a vista of marvelous truth of which we were before entirely unconscious. What other book can do these things? When we read a book written by man, however interesting it may be, it soon loses its interest and its charm; we do not find new beauties in it as we do in the Bible. Its treasures are soon exhausted, but the Bible is ever new, and so I do not believe that the Bible is man's book nor that it could be man's book. Its depths are too deep to come from the heart or mind of man; its heights are too great for him to reach; and its wisdom is more than human. It can but be divine.

The Most Loved of All Books

Wherever the Bible goes, people learn to love and to treasure it above all other books combined. It is the one book that people love; it is the treasure that people hold fast even at the risk of their lives. In past ages when wicked rulers tried to keep it from the people, they could not. At the peril of their lives people would have it. They underwent dangers and tortures, and shrank not from anything, that they might possess this wonderful book. It is not for what it claims to be—though it claims much—nor for what men claim for it, but for what it is to the individual himself that it is so dearly loved. There is that in the Bible which endears itself to the human heart, and no other book has that quality. Other books are enjoyed and admired and praised and valued; but the Bible, in this respect, stands in a class by itself.

The educated and the ignorant, the high and the low, all races in all climes, when they learn to truly know the Bible, and when they submit themselves to the God of the Bible, learn to love it and to delight in it and are enriched and blessed by it; and because I too feel this deep love in my heart for the old Book, I believe it. I believe that, in some way, it was made for me by One who knew my needs, and that it corresponds to the very essence of my inner self; and I believe that I could not love it as I do if it were not God's book and if it were not true.

The Most Hated of All Books

Not only is it the best-loved book, but it is also the most-hated book. No other book has had so many nor such bitter enemies. I suppose more books have been written against the Bible than against all other books combined. Men do not hate Shakespeare nor Milton nor Longfellow; they do not hate works on science nor philosophy; they do not hate books of travel or adventure or fiction; they do not hate the other sacred books of the world; they hate only the Bible. Why this hatred? It can be only because they find in the Bible something that they find nowhere else. What they find there is a true picture of themselves, and the picture is not pleasant to look upon, so they turn away their faces and will have nothing to do with it except to vilify and condemn it. They deliberately misrepresent it and write falsehoods about it; they satirize and ridicule it, using all sorts of weapons and all sorts of methods to combat it, and for

only the one reason—that its truth pricks them in their
consciences and they can by no other means escape from
it.

It is judged by a standard far more stringent than
any other book, not excepting the other sacred books. No
critic would think of treating any other book as he treats
the Bible, nor of requiring of any other book what he
requires of the Bible. The more men hate God, the
more they hate his Word; and this has a deep, underlying reason, and that reason, I believe, is that the Bible
is God's book and that in it there is so much of God
himself.

It Has Withstood All Assaults.

But though so bitterly assailed through all the ages,
the Bible has withstood the assaults of all its enemies
and stands victorious still. The Greek philosophers, with
all their skill, were vanquished. The greatest intellects
of modern times find themselves given pause before it.
The sharpest arrows that unbelief could forge have not
pierced it; the assaults made upon it have resulted only
in the destruction of the weapons used. All through the
ages countless theories—religious, philosophic, scientific.
or other—have been used against the Bible, only to fall
in ruins at last before it and to be rejected even by those
who once advocated them. The Bible endures an amount
of criticism that no other book could endure, and instead
of being destroyed, it is only brightened and made better
known. Could such a thing be truly said of error?
Could error endure what the Bible has endured, and
live? It is the law of nature that error is self-destruc-
tive, but that truth can not be destroyed; and according

to this law, the Bible must be true because of its inde-
structibility.

It Tells Me of Myself

My deepest emotions and longings, my highest thoughts
and hopes, are mirrored there, and the more settled inner
workings of conscience are there recorded. It speaks
to me of my secret ambitions, of my dearest hopes, of my
fears, of the love that burns within me. My desires are
pictured in the Book just as I find them working in my
heart. Whatever picture it draws of the human soul I
find within myself, and whatever I find within myself
I find within its pages, and thus I know that it is true.
No man can know me as the Bible knows me nor picture
out my inner self as the Bible pictures me; and since no
work of man could correspond with my inner self as the
Bible corresponds with me, I know that it did not come
from man.

It Is the Book of Conscience

It is as a mirror into which every man, when he looks,
sees himself. It speaks to his conscience, not as a man
speaks, yet with a potency unknown to any other book.
It is preeminently the book of the conscience. Other
books appeal to men's consciences, but not with the appeal of this book. Other books mirror men, but not like
the Bible. In the silent watches of the night, in the lonely depths of the forest, upon the expanse of the sea, or
wherever man may be, how frequently is it the case that
this book speaks into his conscience in a silent yet thun-
dering voice, and before it he is awed and silenced and
oftentimes terror-stricken. It speaks to the conscience

as only God can speak, and therefore it must be God's book.

It Gives Comfort and Hope

To what book do those in sorrow turn? To Voltaire? to Ingersoll? to Haeckel? Do they turn to science or philosophy or poetry or fiction? There is but one book that is the book of comfort. The sad and desolate heart turns to its pages, and as it reads, the consolation of the Holy Spirit, which fills the book, comes into that heart, and it is comforted. It is as the balm of Gilead; it is as a letter from home to the wanderer; it is as a mother's voice to the child. Friends may speak words to comfort us, but they can not comfort us as does the Book; its words seem to enter into our innermost sorrows with a healing touch. God is the God of all comfort, and it is the comforting God in this comforting book that comforts the soul.

It is also the book of hope. Sometimes man despairs, and he looks here and there for hope, finding none; but there is one book in which hope may always be found. It always has something to offer him to inspire hope with new courage. Therefore it is the hope of the hopeless; since in the troubled soul it brings a calm, brightening dull eyes and causing them to look beyond. It lifts up the bowed head, strengthens the feeble knees, renews the courage, and takes the sadness out of the voice; it is therefore truly the book of hope.

The Book of the Dying

A soldier, desperately wounded, lay in a trench. The shells were bursting around him; the bullets and shrapnel were whistling through the air; the roar of the guns shook the ground. He was going down into the valley of the shadow of death. Knowing that he must pass over to the other side, he reached into his pocket with his little remaining strength and pulled therefrom a soldier's Testament. Handing it to a comrade he said, "Read to me." His comrade opened the book and began to read—"In my Father's house are many mansions: if it were not so I would have told you. I go to prepare a place for you. And if I go and prepare a place for you, I will come again, and receive you unto myself; that where I am, there ye may be also." A smile overspread the face of the dying soldier as he listened to the words amid that solemn and terrible scene. He closed his eyes and lay quite still smiling, then he murmured, "It is well." And with a smile still upon his face he passed across to the other side.

For what book do the dying call? For just any book? What words do they wish to hear in the final hour? There is but one book for that hour; but one that can throw light into that shadowy valley. That is the Bible. It is the book of the living and of the dying, the book of the sorrowing and of the hopeless. It is just such a book as the loving Father would give to the children whom he loves, and it meets their need in all the details of their lives as only God could meet it, and therefore I can but believe that it is the book of God.

Only Answer to the Enigma of Life

The "why" of life is found nowhere else. Other books tell us many truths about life, yet its depths and meaning find expression and answer in only one book. It interprets life; and he who reads the interpretation knows that it is true because it is the story of himself, and in himself is the witness of its truth. Men have sought everywhere the secret of life and the things that pertain thereto, but everywhere, save in the Bible, they find only darkness and obscurity and uncertainty. The Bible, however, speaks in no uncertain terms. It speaks the language of him who knows, and if we reject its voice we are left in a tangled maze, out of which we can not find our way.

The Bible outlives all its critics and is triumphant when they are forgotten; it has many times been pronounced dead, but still it lives; it has been called "exploded," but its power is not dissipated; it has seen all antagonistic theories of the past, one by one, destroyed and rejected, but it still stands in spite of the critics, in spite of its enemies; and those who anchor their faith upon it need not fear what voice is raised against it. Neither need they fear what weapons are brought to bear upon it; for it is truth, and those who fight against it fight against God and are themselves ruined.

It is adapted to all people of every race and clime, to the high and the low, the rich and the poor, the learned and the ignorant. Of no other book can this be said. It is the Book of books, the book of God. In it God speaks, and my inmost heart knows that it is the voice of my Beloved, and leaps for joy.

TALK FOUR

HE MAKETH ME TO LIE DOWN

The Psalmist says of the Lord, his Shepherd, "He maketh me to lie down in green pastures," or, as the Hebrew has it, "in pastures of tender grass." What a world of significance there is in this little sentence: "The Lord is my shepherd."

"He maketh me to lie down." He doth not compel me. That is not the Lord's method; he findeth a better way. If he compelled me to lie down, there would be no pleasure in it. When a sheep is compelled to lie down, it is in fear; it can not but dread what is to happen to it. So the Lord doth not compel me. He leadeth me in the pastures of tender grass, and I eat until I am satisfied, and being satisfied with the sweet and luscious pasturage, I lie down, content. While the sheep is hungry, it will not lie down in the pasture; it desireth to eat. But when it hath eaten its fill, it lieth down and resteth and is satisfied. So he feedeth my soul day by day; the good things of his kingdom doth he give unto me. He satisfieth my soul with fatness. My soul desireth nothing more than what he giveth. If I hunger, he hath a supply, and he giveth me, and that with a generous hand. He knoweth all my needs. He supplieth every one, that I may be "fat and flourishing, to show that the Lord is upright."

There are many enemies about, but "he maketh me to lie down." I am in quietness. My heart is not afraid. The Shepherd standeth between me and those ravening wolves. The lion and the bear can not harm me, for the Shepherd standeth as my protector. His eye shall watch while I lie down. His ear shall hearken and shall hear the sound of their footsteps if they come near. I trust the Shepherd; therefore my heart is not afraid, and I shall lie down safely. It is trust that enableth me to lie down. If I were afraid, I could not thus rest. I should be watching and fearing and trembling. Every noise would alarm me. I should forget about the green pastures. I should forget the tender grass. But he is watching. He hath his weapon in his hand. He doth not fear my enemies, and while he is watching I do not fear them, for he is strong and mighty. He is greater than my foes. They know it and are afraid. They tremble at his voice. They flee away, but I lie safely. He hath said, "I will feed them in a good pasture, and upon the high mountains of Israel: . . . in a fat pasture shall they feed upon the mountains of Israel."

"He leadeth me beside the still waters." When I grow thirsty, the river lieth at the foot of the mountain, and down the slope he will lead me, and there in the shade, in the quiet, restful coolness, I shall drink of the waters of quietness and shall be satisfied, and my soul shall delight in him. The path down which he leadeth me may be steep; there may be thorns along the way; but so long as I permit him to lead me where he will, he will lead me safely. I must not choose my own way. I must not run ahead of him. I must not leave the path. I must follow close to him. I must listen to his voice, and then he will lead me to the still waters, and there I shall rest in his love. Then as the evening falleth, he will lead me to his fold, and inside its walls of security I shall rest during the hours of the night. I shall not fear the darkness, for the Shepherd is watching. I shall not fear the wild beasts round about, for they can not harm me. He will watch over me and bear me up when I am weak. I can rest secure. My shepherd is the Good Shepherd. He loveth his sheep. They are a pleasure to him.

Though he sometimes may needs lead by a rugged way, yet I am safe, for he careth for me. He will lead me in the way that I should go. He will enrich my soul with his goodness. Yea, "goodness and mercy shall follow me all the days of my life; and I will dwell in the house of the Lord forever."

TALK FIVE

BLIGHTED BLOSSOMS

In our yard, a few feet from the door, stands an apple-tree. In the early spring I watched its swelling buds from day to day. Soon they burst forth into snowy blossoms, beautifying the tree, and filling the air with their fragrance. There was the promise of a bountiful crop of fruit. In a few days the petals had fallen like a belated snow. As the leaves unfolded and grew larger. there appeared here and there a little apple that gave promise of maturing into full-ripened fruit. But, alas! how few apples there were compared with the number of blossoms with which the boughs had been laden! Most of the blossoms had been blighted, and had fallen to the ground leaving nothing behind.

"Ah," thought I, "how like these blighted blossoms are so many of the desires and hopes and plans of our lives! How many of our aspirations are never realized! How many of our plans fail! How scanty the perfectly matured fruit in our lives, when compared with the blossoms!" When we consider this, how barren our lives often seem! How little we seem to accomplish! How little our lives seem to amount to!

Every truly saved heart longs to serve. The redeemed heart loves, and love finds its joy in service. How much there is to be done all around us! and how eagerly we would take up the task of doing it! How much we want to accomplish for the Lord! but ah, how little we do really accomplish! How many blossoms of desire we possess! but how little fruit of real accomplishment! Seeing this, we sometimes become discouraged. It does not seem worth while to try to do the few little things that we actually can do. Do the best we can, so many of our blossoms will be blighted—so many of our plans will fail; so many of our hopes will not be realized; so many of our desires will not be fulfilled. We can rejoice in those that are brought to fruitage; we can rejoice in those that do mature; but how about the blossoms that fall and seem to leave nothing behind them? Do they bud in vain? Do they serve no good purpose in our lives? They are not in vain. The blossoms on that apple-tree which were blighted, and died, were just as beautiful and just as fragrant as those which bore fruit. They served a very real purpose, and so do the hopes and purposes that we cherish in our hearts, even though we never see their fruitage.

David was a man who loved the Lord, and out of that love came a desire to build the Lord a house. That desire was never realized by David. Making it a reality was left to others. Nevertheless, David's purpose was pleasing to the Lord. In his prayer at the dedication of the temple, Solomon said: ''And it was in the heart of David my father to build an house for the name of the Lord God of Israel. And the Lord said unto David my father, Whereas it was in thine heart to build an house unto my name, thou didst well that it was in thine heart'' (1 Kings 8:17, 18). God did not despise the desire, even though he did not permit David to carry it out. As God was well-pleased with the desire of David to build him a house, so he is well-pleased with those worthy desires and purposes of our hearts that are never carried out. Whether it be circumstances or surroundings that hinder us, whether it be a lack of wisdom or of ability, whether it be the pressure of other duties, or even if God gives the task to some one else, there is, nevertheless, beauty and fragrance in the desire that is in our heart to do him service.

We must not become discouraged and give up hoping and desiring and planning to do something for the Lord, even though so many of our plans fail and our hopes become blighted. We know that it is the sap flowing upward through the tree that produces the beautiful fragrant blossoms. Likewise God knows that it is the love in our hearts that produces the desire for service; and that love is precious in his sight. Do you sometimes feel that there is so little, oh, so little! that you can do for the Lord? Does your life seem to count so little for his kingdom? and do you long to be more useful? That very longing is as the odor of sweet incense before the Lord. If you are prevented from doing the things that you would gladly do, if circumstances shut you in like a hedge, if you seem weak when you would be strong, you can still do something. The more of these blossoms of desire you have, even if they never reach fruition, the more your life is beautified, and the more the Lord is pleased. These unfulfilled desires work to ennoble our character and to enrich us, provided we do not spend our time mourning and lamenting because we can not put them into action.

There is, however, one danger which we must be careful to shun. Sometimes people have their hearts so set on doing some great thing that they miss the little things, the little opportunities that lie close to their hands. Life is made up of a round of little things. The great things only happen at rare intervals. But it is being faithful in the little things that makes us ready for our opportunities for the great things when they come. Christ said "He that is faithful in that which is least is faithful also in much." The little things are not spectacular, they do not attract much attention, but they are the things that make up life; and if we are true in these little things, God will trust us with some greater things by and by. It is not wrong to yearn to do more; but that longing works evil if, in our reaching forward to greater opportunities, we neglect what opportunities we have. It is the fruits we are able to produce, not their blossoms, that count at the harvest.

Let us, therefore, strive to do all that we can; and if we can not do all that we would, let us remember that the blossoms that are blasted are not in vain. They serve their purpose. They are well worth while; and if we go resolutely and stedfastly on, we shall at last hear the Master's voice say to us, "It is good that it was in thine heart." How sweet these words will sound in our ears! How they will soothe our feelings of dis appointment at not having done more! Let us press on, therefore, and not be discouraged because we do not see our hopes and plans realized in this world. Let us be strong and of good courage, knowing that God knows all about it. Let us thank him for such privileges as we have, and make the best of our opportunities.

TALK SIX

MEETING THE LIONS

The Bible recounts some interesting stories of lions. They are interesting, not simply because they are stories of animals, but because there are things in connection with them from which we may draw some very striking lessons. We all remember the story of Daniel—how he was cast into the den of lions, and how during the long watches of the night he sat there in their den unharmed. What was expected to be the tragedy of his life proved to be his most glorious victory. The expected triumph of his enemies was turned into their utter defeat, and Daniel, stronger and more courageous than ever, came forth to continue his service to God.

Samson too had an experience with a lion. As he was going along the road one day he met a lion, and it attacked him. He had no weapons, yet he met it courageously. We are told that "the Spirit of the Lord came mightily upon him, and he rent him as he would have rent a kid." Some time later he was passing that way and found that a swarm of bees had entered the dried carcass of the lion and made their abode there, and he took of the honey and went on his way.

In the thirteenth chapter of 1 Kings we find another lion story. Here a prophet sent of God went to Samaria and prophesied as God had commanded him, and according to the commandment he started back on his way to Judea. God had told him not to eat or drink there, but to go back immediately by a different way from that by

which he came. He started to obey, but sat down to
rest by the wayside. While he was here, another prophet
came and persuaded him to go back and dine with him.
Then, as he went upon his way, a lion met him and
slew him.

The lions of these stories may be likened to our trials.
We meet trials every now and then in life, and some of
them seem very much like lions. They seem very threatening and very dangerous. Sometimes we try to run
away from a trial, but as surely as we do, we meet another in the pathway in which we go. We are certain to
have trials. The important thing is that we meet them
properly. Some people imagine that if they live as they
should they ought not to have trials. But trials often
come when it is no fault of ours. Daniel was not thrown
into the lions' den because he had not lived right or because he had been unfaithful in something. No; it
was his faithfulness that resulted in his meeting the
lions. It will be that way in our lives. If we are
true and loyal to God, that very loyalty is sure to bring
us trials sometimes. Daniel had his choice in the matter.
He could have been disloyal and escaped the lions, but
he chose rather to be loyal and take the full consequences,
whatever they might be. God wants you and me to dare
to be Daniels too. He does not want us to swerve an inch
from the truth in order to evade any sort of trial. If
we are true, and as a result of that trueness a great trial
like being thrown into a den of lions comes upon us, and
every earthly hope seems shut off, and there is no help
from anywhere, what shall we do? Despair? Ah, no.
God will send his angel and shut the lion's mouth for us,

just as he did for Daniel. Dare to be true. God will
stand by you even in the most trying and desperate hour.

It was not a test of his standing true that brought
Samson face to face with the lion. He met the beast just
by accident. He got into the trouble unwittingly. He
had no expectation of it whatever, but the first thing he
knew, he was face to face with it. That is just the way
it happens with us sometimes: we get into a trial without
any seeming reason for it; we are not expecting anything
of the kind.

If the prophet in Samaria had gone in the way that
God commanded him, he would not have met the lion
that slew him. It was his disobedience that caused the
trouble. Sometimes when we are in trials, we realize
that it is our own fault that we are tried. Sometimes we
may be disobedient, sometimes we may be careless, sometimes it may be this or that; but whatever it is, we realize that it is our own fault. That makes the trial harder
to bear. But however trials come, whatever is their
cause, we must meet them. We have no choice in the
matter. The important thing is to meet them right.
Daniel knew that he had done right and pleased God;
and, furthermore, he met his trial with a calm peace and
full assurance that God would take care of him, and God
did take care of him, and he came through the trial.
He was peaceful through the trial and triumphant after
it, because God was his helper.

Some one has said that our trials make or mar us.
This is true. Either we come out of them stronger than
we went in or we come out of them weaker. We have
either joy or sorrow from them. We should meet our

trials as Samson met the lion. Face them boldly. Do not run or shrink. If you seem to have no adequate weapon to use against them, trust in God and meet them boldly anyway. That is the way Samson did, and do you remember what happened? Why, after a while he got honey out of the carcass. Do you want honey out of your trials? You would rather have that than bitterness. Well, you may have the honey if you will face the trial and overcome it. Conquer in the name of Christ. Do not whimper or whine; do not lament or murmur; do not fear or tremble. Face your trials boldly, and the Spirit of the Lord will come mightily upon you as it did upon Samson, and you will conquer. And then, ah, it is then that the sweetness will come: after you have mastered the trial, in the days that follow, sweetness will come, and you will bless God that he ever permitted you to be so severely tried.

Conflict must always precede victory. The lion must be killed before the bees can build the honeycomb in the carcass. So face your trials boldly and kill them. Then you may taste the sweets of victory. This is the only way, and you are not too weak to take this way. God has promised that he will not suffer you to be tempted above what you are able to bear. If you will believe it and do your part, God will do his, and you will triumph.

TALK SEVEN

EGG-SHELL CHRISTIANS

You have sometimes heard it said of people that "they have to be handled like eggs"; eggs must be handled carefully, or you are likely to break them. Some people are super-sensitive: you have to be very careful what you do or say, or they will be hurt or offended; you can never be sure how they are going to take anything. Such people are much of the time suffering from wounded feelings, are displeased and offended. It is true that some are of a highly nervous temperament and naturally feel things more keenly than others, but it is not this natural nervous sensitiveness that leads to the results above men- tioned, it is a morbid and unnatural state into which people allow themselves to enter. The natural feelings may need restraint and careful cultivation, but these morbid feelings need to be got rid of.

Sometimes people can bear to hear others ridiculed or talked about in a gossiping way, or see them slighted, and think nothing of it or even be amused; but when they themselves become the target for such things, it almost kills them, or at least they feel almost killed. What makes this great difference in their feelings? Why do they feel for themselves so much more than they do for others? Trace the feeling back to its origin, and you will find that their self-love is the thing that has been hurt. If they loved others as they love themselves, they would feel just as much hurt by that which was directed against the other as by that which was directed at themselves. It is self-love that makes people easily offended and easily wounded; and the more self-love they have, the easier they are hurt and the quicker their resentment is aroused. Self-love begets vanity; it quivers in keenest anguish at a sneer or a scornful smile; it is distressed by even a fancied slight. Self-love throws the nerves of sensation all out to the surface and makes them hyper-sensitive, and so the person feels everything keenly. He is constantly smarting under a sense of injustice. He feels he is constantly being mistreated.

Oh, this self-love! How many pains it brings! how many slights it sees! how often it is offended! Reader, are you a victim of self-love? If you are so sensitive, always being wounded and offended, self-love is what is the trouble. If you will get rid of this self-love, you will be rid of that morbid sensitiveness; that is, you will get rid of that morbid sensitiveness that makes people have to be so careful with you.

Self-love makes a person wonder what others are thinking and saying about him. It makes him suspicious of others, suspicious that they are saying or thinking things that would hurt his feelings if known. If two others talk in his presence and he can not hear what is said, he is afraid lest the talk is about him or he is hurt because he is not taken into the confidence of the others. If others are invited to take part in something while he is omitted, he feels slighted and hurt, and can hardly get over it. I have often heard people make remarks like this: "We shall have to invite So-and-so, or he will feel hurt." Self-love is a tender plant; it is easily injured. We may make all sorts of excuses for such sensitiveness; but if we will clear away these excuses and dig down to the root of the trouble, we shall find that God has it labeled "self-love."

Another thing that increases sensitiveness is holding a wrong mental attitude toward others. This attitude manifests itself in a lack of confidence in the good intent of others. If we are looking for and expecting slights, ridicule, and like things, it means we take it for granted that others are holding a wrong attitude toward us. We do not really believe that they love us and have kindly feelings toward us, or that they will be just and kind and sympathetic in their actions that affect us or relate to us. Have you not seen children who, when one would hurt another and say, "Oh, I did not mean to do it!" the other would retort, "Yes, you did; you just did it on purpose"? There are many older persons who are always ready to say, "It was just done on purpose; they just meant to hurt my feelings!" This is childish, but alas, how many professed Christians hold such an attitude! This is a sure way to destroy fellowship and to take the sweetness out of the association with God's people. It is unjust to our brethren. It is the foe of unity and spirituality. Were it not for self-love, we would not think of attributing to others an attitude different from that which we feel that we ourselves hold toward them.

This self-love crops out in all our relations. It constantly exalts us and as constantly depreciates our brethren. God's saints are animated with a spirit of kindness and brotherly affection for each other, and this does not manifest itself in wounds and slights, and if we are looking for such manifestations it is because we do not believe that they have Christlike feelings toward us. God wants us to have more confidence in our brethren than to be looking for them to misuse us.

If we are looking for slights, we shall see plenty of them—even where none exist. If we are expecting wounds, we shall receive them even when no one intends to wound us. Self-love has a great imagination. It can see a great many evils where none exist. It is like a petulant and spoiled child. I remember one child of whom it was said, "If you just crook your finger at him, he will cry." Thinking that this was an exaggeration, I tried it, and the boy cried. There are some people six feet tall who are hurt just that easily. They are truly "lovers of their own selves." Paul said, "When I became a man, I put away childish things." It is high time others were doing the same thing. Suppose Christ had been as sensitive as you are, would he have saved the world? If Paul had been like you, would he have endured the persecution and dangers and tribulations and misrepresentations that he bore to carry the gospel to the world? He was not so sensitive. He was not looking for slights. He was a real, full-sized man for God. The secret is that he loved Christ and others more than he loved himself; therefore he could endure all things for his brethren's sake, that they might be saved.

The cure for self-love and the sensitiveness that comes from it is to turn your eyes away from self to Jesus Christ, and look upon him until you see how little and insignificant you and your interests really are. Look upon him until you see how high above all such narrow pettishness he was, until you see that his great heart was so overrunning with love for others that he had no time to think of himself. Then ask him to revolutionize you and fill your heart with that same love till your eyes and your thoughts and your interests are no longer centered upon yourself, and self no longer fills your horizon, but your heart goes out to others till it quite draws you away from yourself. You will find this the cure for your sensitiveness; and when you are thus cured, you will no longer be an egg-shell Christian, and people will no longer have to be afraid of wounding or offending you.

TALK EIGHT

TWO WAYS OF SEEING

The appearance that things have to us depends, to a great extent, upon the way that we look at them. Sometimes our mental attitude toward them is largely respon-sible for their appearance. Often two or more persons look at the same thing, and each one sees something quite different from what the others see. Persons who see the same thing will often have very different stories to tell about it afterwards, and will be very differently affected by what they see. This is not because their eyes differ so much, but because their mental attitude affects the interpretation of what they see.

A notable example of this is seen in the twelve spies sent by Moses to spy out the land of Canaan. The Israelites had crossed the Red Sea. Their enemies had been destroyed behind them. They had come at God's command almost to the borders of the Promised Land. Here the people camped while the spies went to see the country. They passed through it and viewed the land and the people, and presently came back with their re-port. It was a wonderful land, they agreed, a land flowing with milk and honey. The samples of the fruit they brought back were large and fine specimens. Of course, the people were at once very eager to possess such a land, but the question came up, *Are we able to do so?* What kind of people are they over there? Are they good fighters? Are they courageous? Do they have strongly fortified cities? As soon as this question was broached, there was a difference of opinion. Caleb said, "Let us go up at once, and possess it; for we are well able to overcome it" (Num. 13:30). The others, however, did not agree with him, except Joshua. They said, "We be not able to go up against the people; for they are stronger than we . . . and all the people that we saw in it are men of a great stature. And there we saw the giants, the sons of Anak, which come of the giants: and we were in our own sight as grasshoppers, and so we were in their sight" (vs. 31-33).

Now, what made the difference in their views? They all saw the same things; they all saw the same people; but when it came to telling of them, they told very different stories. The difference must have lain in the men themselves. When the ten saw those sons of Anak, they felt that they were as grasshoppers in comparison with such giants. "Why, we amount to nothing at all," the ten spies thought. "Those great big fellows could walk right over us." And when they recalled their sensations, the land did not seem so fine, either, and they said, "It is a land that eateth up the inhabitants thereof." They did not stop to consider that their own words condemned them. How could a land be such a bad land and yet the people who lived in it be so strong and so great?

Joshua and Caleb, however, were not to be frightened by the stories that the others told. So they said, "The land, which we passed through to search it, is an exceeding good land" (chap. 14:7). They also held fast their confidence in the ability of Israel to gain the land saying, "If the Lord delight in us, then he will bring us into this land, and give it us; a land which floweth with milk and honey. Only rebel not ye against the Lord, neither fear ye the people of the land; for they are bread for us: their defense is departed from them, and the Lord is with us; fear them not'' (vs. 8, 9).

Now, all these men were probably honest. They probably described things just as these appeared to them. What was the difference? The difference was not in their eyes, but in that which was back of their eyes. When the ten went through the land and saw the giants, they forgot all about God. It was themselves against the giants, with God left out; and when we leave God out, things look very different. How big those giants looked! ''We poor grasshoppers had better be getting out of here quickly. We do not stand any show at all,'' they thought. ''How could Israel fight with such fellows, anyway?'' The ten were full of doubts, and they looked through their doubts, and their doubts magnified the Anakim.

But Caleb and Joshua had no doubts. They had faith in God—faith that did not waver. They remembered the Red Sea. They remembered the manna from heaven. They remembered the other things that God had done They looked at the situation through their faith; and instead of feeling as if they were grasshoppers, they felt themselves more than a match for the giants. The two were not at all frightened. ''Why,'' they said, in effect, when they came back, ''they will be only bread for us. We shall just eat them up. They have heard what God has done among us, and they are too scared to fight. Their defense is departed from them.'' Then these men of faith began talking about the other side. "The Lord is with us; fear them not. What do those fellows amount to, since God is not with them? What do their fortresses amount to? Let us go up at once," said they. "Why, we can whip them with ease."

But the people listened to both sides, and their ears heard; but instead of listening through their faith to Joshua and Caleb, they listened through their doubts to the ten and believed them and became very much frightened; and in consequence they went to murmuring and complaining because Moses had brought them out there to face such a situation. The result was that they were turned back, defeated by their enemies, and had to wander forty years in the wilderness until all the old ones perished.

Now, that is just the difference between faith and doubts. Looking back from the present time, we can easily believe that God would have conquered the land before them. Yes, we can believe that. We can see how foolish it was for them to turn back and to be afraid and to murmur. That all looks very plain to us now. We say, "How foolish and how full of unbelief they were!" But the question is, Are we doing any better than they did? When we look at the obstacles in our way, when we look at the troubles that seem to be coming, when we look at the things that are before us, do we look through faith, like Caleb and Joshua, or do we look through doubts, like the ten? Do your trials and difficulties make you feel like a grasshopper? Does it seem that you would surely be overwhelmed? Does it look as though you could never get through, that you might as well give up? If so, you are looking at things through your doubts just as the ten did.

The people who win, the people who are victorious. are those who look at things through their faith. They do not compare their troubles and trials and difficulties with themselves; they compare these with God. They behold God's greatness. They behold the things that he has done in the past. They see how he has helped others. They see that they have been helped in the past, that God has stood right by them and helped them through. They get their faith and their eyes working together, and then they can see a way out of their difficulties, just as Caleb did. "They shall be bread for us," faith says. "No use to be afraid. Giants don't count. What is a giant beside God?" Doubts say, "Oh, what shall we do?" Faith takes a new grip on its sword and says, "Come on; let's go and conquer them."

Your eyes are all right; they will see things all right, but the question is, What is behind your eyes—doubts, or faith? That is the thing that really counts. Doubts will magnify your troubles, will make them look very great. Doubts will make your power look very small. They will make your ability to fight look as nothing They will make you feel like running or surrendering. Faith will not work that way. It will fill you with courage; it will put the song of victory in your heart. Get faith behind your eyes. Look out by faith. Remember that God will fight your battles. Be strong and of a good courage, and you will overcome your foes. But doubts will spoil things for you. Doubts will take away what

courage you have. Doubts will ruin you if you let
them. So get rid of your doubts. Look to God, believe
in him, trust in him, and the victory will be yours.
Take your stand with Caleb and Joshua. Do you remember what became of the spies? The ten doubters died in
the wilderness, and their bodies were left there; but
the two who had faith went on into the Promised Land
and died full of years and of honors.

TALK NINE

THE LIVING BIBLE

The Bible is a living book. What it is to us depends on what we are to it. If we approach it with unbelief and sneers, it shudders like a wounded thing and closes up its heart, and we gaze only on a cold and gross exterior. We behold the form of its words, but discern not the treasures hidden in them. It appears cold and life-less and repellent, and we go away depressed and unbelieving.

If we approach it reverently, trustfully, and confidently, it opens up to us its hidden depths. It shows to us its wonders. We may see in it unequaled beauties, unfading glories, magnificent vistas of thought; we may hear its voice of love, tender beyond words; we may feel the warmth of its affection, be uplifted by its hopefulness, and thrilled with the tones of its joy-bells.

If we open to it our heart's door and pour out our treasures of affection, it in turn opens to us a great storehouse, and we may eat and be satisfied, and drink and thirst not. We may revel in its rich perfume, the rythmic cadences of its music, the splendor of its heavenly light, and to us there is no question whether it is the living truth.

The Bible is to the Christian what the forest is to him who delights in nature. He who walks through the forest laughing, talking, and singing, hears not the sweet notes of the songster nor sees the wild things. He who would see and hear the things that delight the nature-lover must steal softly and silently along, watching his footsteps, hiding in the shadows, and thus he may see nature as she is. Likewise he who comes to the Bible full of self-importance with mind and heart self-centered sees not the natural beauty of the Bible. We must come to it effacing self, seeking not our own but the things of Christ, and we shall find it a mine of spiritual gold, a fountain of living water, a balm for every sorrow, a light in every dark hour—the one and only book that meets and satisfies the needs of the human soul.

TALK TEN

HEEDING INTUITIONAL WARNINGS

There are things which we know and feel but which do not result from our own study. We have a consciousness that there is some supreme power over us, and we are conscious of a certain responsibility to, and a dependence upon, this higher power. Reading the Bible and reasoning may give us clearer ideas of this power and our relations to it, but we have the consciousness of its existence without being taught.

This is never more clearly seen than in the case of the man who denies the existence of a personal God. As surely as he rejects the God of the Bible, he sets up something else in His place, and though he may call it by some other name than God, he will, nevertheless, attribute to it the powers and actions that belong to God. These intuitions by which we know without being conscious of how we know are given us by God for our protection and safety, and we ought to give careful heed to their testimony.

Sometimes our reason sees no harm in a thing, but we do not feel just right about it. A doctrine may look ever so plausible and be ever so interesting; but if we feel an inward uneasiness after consideration of it, there is a reason why we should be careful. Our intuition will often detect something wrong when our reason has not yet done so. These intuitions are not to be disregarded. They are God's means of warning us against unseen dangers.

Sometimes when we come in contact with people, we see nothing outwardly wrong, but we have an inward feeling that all is not well. We feel that there is some·thing wrong somewhere, even though we may be at a loss to know what it is. Sometimes we come in contact with a company of people and at once feel a strange something that we can not analyze; but we can not always trust our feelings. There are many things that influence us, and it is very easy to misinterpret them. Nor should we conclude that there is something very badly wrong with any one merely because we have peculiar feelings when in his presence. There may be something wrong, however, and it behooves us to be on our guard. Sometimes it happens that such feelings arise when we are in the presence of people who are deeply tried, or discouraged, or suffering under the assaults of Satan.

There are many evil spirits at work in these days among professors of religion, and especially is this true among the various holiness factions. Have you ever gone into a meeting and felt that some way you did not "fit" there? The worshipers may have seemed joyful and may have said many good things, but all the while you felt an inward uneasiness. There was some reason for this, and whether the reason was spiritual or merely human, it was wise to exercise carefulness. It is usually best to refrain from trying to make yourself blend with anything when you have that internal sense of protest against it.

Fellowship is natural and spontaneous. It can not be forced. If you are straight and true and your heart is

open and unprejudiced, you will usually have fellowship
with whatever is of God. Most sectarian holiness people
are so broad that they can take in almost anything and
call it good. Beware of this spirit. God's Spirit accepts
only the good. If you have ease and freedom with true,
established, spiritual people of God, and are free in
meetings where the whole truth is preached and the
Spirit of God works freely, and then when you come in
contact with other professors you fail to have that freedom, do not accuse yourself nor try to force yourself
to have fellowship with them.

A preacher once came into a certain community and
began to preach. He was quite enthusiastic; he praised
the Lord and shouted. He preached much truth and
professed to be out clean for God. It was afterwards
discovered that he was very crooked and wholly unworthy
of confidence. I asked a number of the congregation
later how it came that they received him. Their answer
was that, as he came recommended by some good brethren and preached so much truth, when they did not feel
right about him they came to the conclusion that they
must be wrong and he right. So they accused themselves
and went on through the meeting suffering under a heavy
burden. They knew they had no such feelings when
other ministers came into their midst, nor did they feel
that way in their own ordinary meetings. But in spite
of this, they took the wrong course, and the result was
that the congregation received much harm both spiritually and financially. The same thing happened with
this preacher in other places, till at length he came to
a place where some refused to ignore their feelings or to

accuse themselves of being in the wrong. Instead, they sent at once for two well-established ministers, and as soon as they came into the community, the crooked preacher fled and was seen no more in those parts. Sometimes some one will come around making a high profession, and while we can see nothing wrong, we do not feel free with him, or, in other words, we have a sense of uneasiness. We feel at home with other saints, but not so with this person. Beware. If you are in fellowship with those whom you know to be true saints, look out for those with whom you do not have inward harmony. Do not blame yourself nor disregard the warning. Isolated Christians naturally become hungry for spiritual association. Sometimes they go to meetings where, while they find some good things, they also see other things and feel things that grate upon their spiritual sense of propriety. In such cases one should be guarded and should not try to "fit" with these things. To blend with them you must become like them; and if you become like them when they are not right, you will find that when you come into an assembly where the truth and Spirit have freedom, you will not blend there. If you ignore those inner warnings and accept something contrary to them, you will soon find yourself out of harmony with God's church and without the liberty you used to have among the children of God.

Do not follow your intuitions blindly, but do not go contrary to them. Let your reason find out the way of action before you act, so that you may act wisely. But when that inward sense says to us, "Stop, look, listen," we shall do well to heed its warning.

TALK ELEVEN

DOING SOMETHING WORTH WHILE

We all like to feel that what we are doing counts for something, that it is really worth while. We like to see practical results. We know that much labor is lost in the world, and we do not want ours to be lost. The ordinary things of life seem to amount to so little. They are not spectacular; no one pays very much attention to them; and we naturally feel that when we do something, we want it to be something that people can see and that they will think is worth while, and something that we ourselves can feel is worth while. Some think: "If I could just preach, I shouldn't mind working for the Lord. But, oh! I can do so little—nothing worth while at all, nothing worth the effort. What can my feeble efforts accomplish, anyway?"

Others think that if they could go to a foreign land and work among the heathen, draw people to Christ there, send back home great reports of what they have accomplished, have their names published in the paper, and have people talking about them, then that would be worth while. But since they are only ordinary people and can do only ordinary things, it seems to them that it hardly pays to try. They will just follow the line of least resistance and do things the easiest way. Of course they want to do what they can for God, but they want to do something really worth while.

And now, reader, what is really worth while in life? Is it only those things that make a great show? is it only

those things that the world counts great? A sister said
to me recently in a letter, "I used to think that I could
do nothing worth while, but I have found that just
simply living salvation before people is a great work."
Now, that sister has learned a wonderful lesson. She has
found a truth so great that most people do not recognize
it as truth when they do find it. It is one of those truths
that have the peculiarity of seeming small and insignificant though they are the very fundamentals of truth.

Just simply living salvation before people—yes, that
is what counts, and it counts more than anything else.
That is one of the very greatest things that an individual
has ever done in this world. Talk is cheap, and many
people can talk all day and say scarcely anything either.
Some people can sway great crowds by their eloquence,
they can accomplish wonderful things, but still they can
not live salvation, or, at least, they do not. There is no
power so great in this world as the simple power of a
holy, quiet life. The sister mentioned can never hope to
do great things as other people might count them. She is
in frail health; she is isolated from other saints and can
not attend meetings as can many others; she has not
the ability to preach or to do anything very great, as
greatness is usually reckoned; but she has learned the
great fact that she is not shut out from doing a grand
work.

If all God's people could learn this lesson—if they
could learn that it really counts just simply to live right,
just simply to be an ordinary every-day Christian; if
they could once get that thoroughly fixed in their minds
and hearts—it would glorify their lives, it would exalt

the common service, it would shed a halo over their lives, and they would not feel discouraged.

When Moses was at Pharaoh's court, I suppose he thought that he was doing something really worth while. He amounted to something there. But when the Lord let him be driven, or rather frightened, away from that court and he went out into the wilderness, I suppose he thought his occupation there was hardly worth while. Why, what was he doing, anyway? Just taking care of the sheep, leading them out in the morning to the pasture, bringing them back to the fold at night, seven days in the week—just doing this and nothing more. I suppose it did not look very big to Moses, but it did to God. God thought it worth so much that he kept him at that work for forty years. Then Moses, at the age of eighty, when it looked as if he were about done with this world, was called to go to do something for the Lord. That forty years in the wilderness counted now. It had given him experience that helped to qualify him for the work to which God had called him. He came out of there worth while because he had done something worth while in those years. He had learned about God—oh, so many things he had learned! and now he was ready to put that knowledge into practise.

Sometimes we have wilderness periods in our lives, when God lets us be shut up in a corner, as it were, and do the little things that do not seem to count. But they count on us if they do not count anywhere else. There is one thing—and just one—that stands out above all other things in the human life, and that is faithfulness. No matter what our life may be, nor where we may be,

nor what is our situation, if we are just faithful it is sure
to count, and to count a great deal. That is one thing
that you can do: you can be faithful to the Lord. You
can do what he wants you to do. You can live pure,
holy, undefiled, and keep shining every day, no matter
what the circumstances may be. Just remember to keep
shining. That is the thing that counts. Keep living
clean and as God wants you to live. If you do this,
he will know where he can find somebody who is faithful
when he wants something else done. But ever keep this
before you: there is no greater nor more necessary work
in the world than putting the truth of God into visible
form in a pure and quiet life.

TALK TWELVE

HOME-MADE CLOUDS

Louise stood looking out of the window with unseeing eyes. There was a troubled expression upon her face. There were tears in her eyes, and a lump in her throat. What was the trouble? An hour before she had been singing as blithely as a song-bird. Her morning devotions had been sweet. The presence of God had been with her. The day had started out full of sunshine, but alas! now her sky was clouded.

It had all happened in a moment. Her younger brother had been playing with his dog and had carelessly run against the stand upon which her flower-pots were sitting and had upset one of the choice plants, breaking the pot and ruining the flower. Louise saw the happening. How careless it was of the boy! Quickly a feeling of impatience arose, and before she realized what she was doing, she had spoken sharply to her brother and had said hasty words that she immediately regretted. Her conscience quickly reproved her. She felt bad over the loss of the flower, but she felt much worse over her hasty words. A dark, heavy cloud settled down upon her. The sunshine was all gone; there was no longer any song in her heart, but heaviness instead.

Standing there by the window, she now meditated over it. Oh, if she had been more tender! If she had only exercised more self-control! If she had kept back those hasty words! It was quite true that Tom had been very careless. Still, she knew that he too loved the flowers.

He did not mean to destroy one. Louise loved Tom, and because of this she felt all the more deeply what she had done. He was gone now, she knew not where. She would be glad to apologize to him and beg his pardon if he were there. She decided that she would tell him as soon as he returned, and that gave her some satisfaction, but it did not take away the cloud. She thought of how bright the morning and how light and care-free her heart had been! But now her day was clouded, and worst of all, she had made the cloud herself, by her own haste.

That is often the way it is with us. We make so many of our own clouds in life. Clouds often come over our lives from the actions of others; sometimes they come through circumstances that can not be helped; sometimes they come from Satan himself. Such clouds as these do not have the effect upon us that our home-made clouds do. The things that are hardest to bear are the things that we feel we have brought upon ourselves. These get closer to us than anything else. They have a sting to them that nothing else has. Many times people do things that try us; but if we also do or say something hastily at that time, it will increase our trial and make it the more difficult to bear. It will make the clouds that come all the darker. If we have not been as kind as we ought to have been, if there has been a sharpness in our words, or if we have manifested our displeasure at something in a way that showed our feelings too much, it is sure to bring a cloud over our day.

The more tender our consciences, the more we shall feel these things and the more the tendency will be to cloud our days. It is true that we shall feel displeased over things, and it is very natural to manifest our displeasure in some way. Some people are very impulsive and speak before they stop to think what they are saying or what the result will be, and thus they are continually making clouds for themselves. There are times when we must resolutely take hold of ourselves when the feeling of displeasure comes, as it is sure to do. The will must grapple with these emotions quickly and not let them get into action. Our wills were given us to rule ourselves with. When tempted to be unkind or to be hasty in our words and actions, we should say within ourselves: "I will not speak hasty words. I will control myself and keep sweet. I will be patient; I will be kind. I will do as the Lord would have me to do." Then we should put these resolutions quickly into action. Instead of the trial bringing a cloud over us, the fact that we have conquered ourselves and kept ourselves in the attitude that we should hold toward God and toward others will make the sunshine all the brighter.

Conquer yourself; set a watch before your lips. If you are of an impulsive disposition, you may fail again and again, but do not be discouraged, keep up the fight. You will win in the end. You will reach at last the place where self-control acts automatically, where you will think in time. If you fail and the clouds come, endure them patiently, resolving to do better the next time. Do not let yourself be crushed under the circumstance. Do not let yourself be so discouraged that you think that there is no use in trying, that you never will overcome. Keep up the fight; you will yet come out conqueror.

Sometimes people feel that God is leading them to do

a certain thing; they feel strongly impressed to do it. They see an opportunity; then, perhaps through timidity or indecision, they let the opportunity pass by, and when it is gone they feel bad because they failed to improve it. How they regret not having done it! If they had another opportunity, they would not let it slip. But it has gone. In vain do they wish for it again. They have failed, and that failure brings a dark cloud over them. It is another home-made cloud. They can not blame any one else for it—not even Satan. But they do blame themselves, and sometimes to such an extent that it takes the joy and sweetness out of the day, and possibly out of several days. If we have done such things, it does no good to heap reproaches upon ourselves. That only makes our clouds darker. The way out is to open our hearts to God and tell him all about it, asking him to help us to be more courageous, more diligent to take advantage of our opportunities, and more faithful to follow his leadings. Let us resolve in our hearts that we will do this, then go cheerfully about it.

Frivolous or foolish conversation or actions sometimes bring clouds over our sky. The Spirit reproves us and we see our fault. To chide and condemn ourselves does no good. The only profitable thing for us to do at such times is to be open-hearted and frank toward the Lord and tell him about it, to ask his help that we may do better the next time, and to determine in our hearts that we will do better. I do not mean that we should get into bondage. God wants us to be free, to live naturally, and not to live under a strain, but to exercise a proper degree of caution.

I suppose we all have regrets and come more or less short of our ideals at times. But if we are as careful and as true as we ought to be, we shall not have so many of these home-made clouds; but if we do have them, let us bear up patiently. It will do no good to chastise ourselves. The only thing we can do that will be profitable is to trust in the Lord, and go ahead until the darkness passes away and the sun shines again. Let us be true to God and hold fast our confidence and our decision to serve him and be ready to confess our faults before him. He will treat our faults as faults, not as sins. He will not cut us off for such things. He will have mercy upon us and will show his loving-kindness toward us. Let us therefore trust in him and make as few of these home-made clouds as possible.

TALK THIRTEEN

IT PLEASED THE LORD TO BRUISE HIM

It is a mystery in the minds of many, why Christian people often have to suffer. With all the promises of physical healing, they still are many times in pain, notwithstanding God's faithfulness and his omnipresence. They also suffer temptations, persecutions, and soul-conflicts. How can we explain these things? How can we harmonize these with the teachings of a loving God? When we read Paul's experience, we find it largely a record of privation and suffering, of sorrow and heaviness. It is true that in it all there is a note of joy and an unquenchable shout of victory, but nevertheless soul, mind, and body often had to endure the lash of pain. Did God love him? Why, then, must such things be?

God loved Christ with a perfect love, but we read that· "although he had done no violence, neither was any deceit in his mouth, yet it pleased Jehovah to bruise him; he hath put him to grief" (Isa. 53: 9, 10, A. S. V.). What strange language! He had done no evil, he was guilty of nothing, and yet "it *pleased* the Lord to bruise him." Is it true that love is tender, the tenderest of all things, and yet can bruise and find pleasure in it? But this is just what happened. Jesus, the innocent Lamb of God, was "smitten, stricken of God." When we remember Gethsemane, the crown of thorns, the cruel cross, it does not seem an act of love for God to give his Son over to such suffering; yet it was love, truest love. Why did God thus deal with him? It was not because the Father-heart did not feel that agony. It was the only means to an end, and love desired that end so much that it pleased it to make the great sacrifice that out of it might come the infinite joy of a world's redemption.

There is nothing that brings Christ so close to men as his sufferings; there is nothing that makes men trust in him so much as the story of those last days. If that story were taken from the pages of the Bible, what would Christ be to us? Only a great teacher whose morality was high and wonderful, though to us unattainable; but with this record added, he becomes a Savior and makes his righteousness attainable by us all. Had he not suffered, he could not have brought us to God. How much poorer we should be today without the story of Gethsemane and Calvary, without knowing that "it pleased the Lord to bruise him" and that out of his sighs and tears and groans has flowed into our hearts a fountain of joy and love and tenderness whereby we have been enriched and the angels of God have been caused to sing a song for joy!

If God was pleased to bruise his own beloved Son, need we marvel if he is sometimes pleased to bruise us? If we are sometimes bowed down with grief, if anguish takes hold upon us, if the sky grows dark above us, and if God seems to have turned away, is it any proof that he no longer loves us? Is it not only the proof that God sees something to be accomplished that can be accomplished in no other way, and that he is pleased for the sake of that gain to let us suffer? The things that are worth while come through pain. Joy does not make us stronger nor bring us nearer God; nor does it refine, ennoble, or enrich us. The pure gold comes from the fire only and the tempered steel also must have passed through the flame. God would have us pure as gold and as strong as steel, and to have us so he can not spare the flame. We must pass through the furnace of afflic- tion. We are told that God "doth not afflict willingly nor grieve the children of men" (Lam. 3:33). It is only that something may come out of it that will be better and more blessed than could have been without it.

We know in reality only what we know by experience. Those who would be instruments in God's hands to help others must often have a preparatory training-course in the school of suffering; how else could they know how to help others? Brother, sister, has God called you to do a work for him? If so you need not marvel if he lets the rod of pain be laid upon you. If you have hin- drances which seem to shut up the way before you, if you have trials that you can not understand, if you have disappointments and perplexities, if you have spiritual conflicts that threaten to overwhelm you, do not think it strange. How can you teach others how to bear such things if you have not borne them? How can you know the way out for others if you have never gone that way? How can you teach others to look for the blessings in these things if you have not their fruitage in your own life? Those who have suffered most can enter most into the sufferings of others.

The successful worker will find that the strength and wisdom that bring him success was the gift of pain, and had not pain brought him strength and knowledge, success could not now be his. Likewise sometimes we must suffer for others if we would save them. So if you would be a worker for God and know how to enter truly into the sorrows and needs of others, you must yourself drink the bitter cup and feel the chastening rod.

After the Lord called me to his work, I endured some great soul-conflicts. In them I suffered inexpressibly. I almost despaired at times, but I look back upon those things now as being the things that made me understand the human heart, that gave me a broader sympathy, and that have since enabled me to enter into the sorrows and needs of others and to minister comfort and help as I could not otherwise have done. Those early sufferings unlocked a thousand mysteries and enriched not only my own life but also the lives of others. Endure these things with patience; for out of them will come to you that which is more precious than gold. If you do not suffer, you can be of little use to those who do suffer. The promise is, "If we suffer with him, we shall also reign with him."

Abraham suffered in that one supreme sacrifice, but his example of faithfulness in the test has enriched mil-lions of souls. Job suffered not only physical agony but the keenest and deepest of spiritual agony, yet that suffering was only an opportunity for God to manifest his mercy and kindness. How much Job learned of God by enduring through these dark days and how much the world has learned! If we should take out of the Bible the record of suffering and its results that are written there, we should take out of it all that is best and noblest and most helpful and encouraging. How much poorer we should be if the sacred record told only of joy and peace and comfort, if it spoke only of victory and achievement, and told us nothing of the hard road that leads up to them! If the Lord chastises us, it is "for our profit"; if God smites, it is only to enrich; so bear with patience, endure as seeing him who is invisible. Be "patient in tribulation," drink the cup of your Gethsemane, wear your thorny crown without complaint, endure your Calvary; for unto you is given both to suffer and to reign with him.

TALK FOURTEEN

PUTTING CLOUDS OVER THE SUN

A little boy was walking down the street rejoicing in the possession of a bright new penny. He was going to buy some candy with it. He could almost taste it already, but just then he dropped his penny upon the sidewalk. An older boy seized it and started off. The little boy began to cry and demanded his penny, but the other boy only laughed derisively. It was a mean trick. It spoiled the whole day for the boy, and ever after when he thinks of the incident, he will have an unpleasant feeling. The older boy put a dark cloud over the little fellow's sun that day, and the shadow will be cast upon him through other days.

A number of persons were sitting in a room talking over a matter. During the conversation one man made a charge against another, comparing him half contemptuously with a man whose conduct had been quite unbecoming. The charge was like a dagger in the man's heart. He knew it was both untrue and unjust. He was conscious of the uprightness of his conduct. He had always held the other man in high esteem, and to be thus publicly wounded by him was almost unbearable. He made no defense, but he went out of that room with an aching heart, humiliated and wronged. His friend had put a great cloud over his sun. Years have passed, but the darkness of that cloud has not yet all passed away. When he thinks of the injustice, there is still a pang in his heart. He does not feel bitter toward the other; he has forgiven; but the close tie has been broken. He has never since been able to confide in the one who did him such an injury.

A faithful minister had labored for years for souls. He had been successful; he had been a blessing to many. One day a certain person spoke of him half jestingly in a manner that aroused the suspicions of some others who were present. These suspicions grew until they became whispers, and the whispers grew till they became open charges. The minister could not prove them to be false. They hindered his labors. They bowed down his head with sorrow. Some one had put a cloud over his sun and over his name, and for years the dark shadow of it rested upon his life.

How easy it is to put a cloud over some one's sun, to make some life dark that might have been bright! It may seem only a little thing, but sometimes a little cloud can make a dark shadow. We may not see either the cloud or the shadow, but the heart that is darkened both sees and feels. How many times parents, by unkind words or actions, becloud their children's sky! One way in which parents do this is by telling the faults of their children to visitors, in the presence of the children. There is scarcely anything more disheartening to a child than this. He feels humiliated and hurt. He feels, and justly feels, that he has been mistreated. It sinks down into his soul and rankles there. It discourages him, and if it is often repeated he comes not to care if he is at fault. Constant reproof and faultfinding make a child's life gloomy and sad. That is not the way to cure faults; it is the way to make them worse.

I once knew a young saint who had a rich experience of salvation. A certain relative who opposed her religion began finding fault with her and kept doing so at every opportunity. The result was that that young life was beclouded and a deep melancholy settled down over her. Her cheerfulness gave way to sadness and moroseness. The song of joy, once so often upon her lips, was stilled. Some one had put a cloud over her sun, and her life was never what it otherwise might have been.

Children may darken the hearts and lives of their parents. How many times is the mother-heart or father-heart grieved by the conduct of the children! It may be that they are only thoughtless, or they may be disobedient and wilful. Young people, cherish your parents, try to make their lives as bright as you can. They have many cares. These are enough for them to bear without your adding a single one. When you have grown older and they have gone out of your life, you may look back with a pang of regret at the times when you caused their hearts to ache. Brighten their lives while you may; then when you look into the open grave where Father or Mother is being laid to rest, your conscience will not smite you.

We are told that "no man liveth unto himself." There is a circle of influence about our lives that affects every other life that we touch. We brighten or darken the lives about us. We lighten or make heavier the burdens of others. Every unkind word or look makes a shadow on some life. Every slighting remark, every sarcastic fling, every contemptuous smile, puts a cloud over somebody's sun. Lack of appreciation has darkened many a life. How much better it would be to take away the clouds, to banish the gloom! You can do this just as easily as you can bring clouds. It is just as easy to speak kind words as to speak unkind ones, and you will feel much better over it yourself. You can encourage and help, you can speak words of appreciation. When people please you, let them know it. When people do well, or even when they try to do well and fail, you can show that you appreciate their efforts. You can be cheerful and courteous and kind. That will make sunshine for others. There are enough clouds in life at best in this world of sorrow. Be a sunshine-bearer. Drop a little good cheer into every life you touch. No matter what you are by nature, you can form the habit of being cheerful and encouraging. Even when you have heavy burdens yourself, you can be encouraging and helpful to others.

Do not let your troubles be mirrored on your face. One's face can smile and his words can be cheery if his own heart does ache. I am not writing a mere theory. I know what pain and gloom and heaviness are. I know what burdens are. During the first few months of my illness every one knew how I felt. My face told the story without words. I finally saw that that would not do, and deliberately set to work to get the gloom out of my face and out of my words. You who read what I write know something of my success. You can do the same.

TALK FIFTEEN
WHAT IS YOUR WORD WORTH?

Everything is measured by some standard of value. Material things are measured by length, breadth, weight, density, usefulness, or intrinsic value. Character also has its standard of measurement. Some people are valued more highly than others, whether in the community, in the church, or in the nation. People are valued, not for their physical size or weight, but for their abilities and more especially for their characters. In a Christian the special thing of value, and the only special thing, is his character. If one's character is not of a higher and better quality than that of people in general, one has no right to the name Christian.

The quality of one's character is indicated in various ways. One's words are generally a clear index to one's character. A person is judged by them, and his value is reckoned by the reliance that may be placed upon his word. We know some on whose word we fully rely. If they tell us anything, we believe them. If they make us a promise, we do not expect it to be broken. We rely upon them because they have shown by their conduct that they themselves place a high value upon their own word. Of such persons it is often said, "If he says it is so, it is true," or, "If he makes a promise, he will fulfil it." Such men wield a strong influence in a community. People can easily believe and trust in their character. It is a sad fact that such individuals are the exception rather than the rule, even among professed Christians. How many times promises are made only to be broken or forgotten! This is a grave matter and marks a serious defect in Christian character. We should never make a promise unless we fully expect to fulfil it, and we ought to feel under deep obligation to keep our promise. If we are careless and neglectful of this, it is sure to lower us in men's esteem, and we shall be cheapened and discredited.

Hasty Promises

Many times promises are made hastily. The person does not stop to consider what he really is promising; he does not weigh its meaning. He says, "Yes, yes, I will"; but later when he thinks the matter over, it looks different to him. He is sorry that he made the promise, and begins to look for some way out so that he will not have to fulfil it.

These hasty promises are just as binding as any others. If we ignore them and do not make our word good, the persons to whom we have made them will have just reason to condemn us. It is easier to make promises than it is to fulfil them. Beware of making haste to promise. Think about the fulfilment. Think whether you really want to do, or really will do, what you promise. Consider your promises binding. Have the fear of God before you just as much in this matter as in other things. If you wish people to value your word, you must show that you value it yourself. If you do not value it enough to keep it, do not expect others to value it. If you value your word, it will make you careful about your promises—careful in making them, careful in keeping them.

Do not make rash promises. Consider what you are promising. Is it something that you can perform? Consider your ability and what things may hinder. Have you any just reason to suppose that you can fulfil it? Would it be wise for you to do it? Would it be best? Have you made other promises that will conflict with it? Remember that when you once promise, if you do not keep your word your failure leaves a shadow upon your character in the mind of the one you promised unless there is some good and sufficient reason to excuse you in his sight.

Do not make careless promises. The Bible tells us that in our planning we should say, "If the Lord will"; that is, we should take into consideration that the unexpected may happen. We do not know the future; therefore we ought not to make our promises too positive. We ought to qualify them so as to allow for hindrances.

We ought to be honest in making our promises. Many promises are made when there is no intention of carrying them out. Many people, rather than to say no, will promise and then refuse to perform, thereby making themselves liars. They have not manhood enough to refuse and honestly tell why, so they make a promise and break it. That is the coward's way out. It is the dishonest way out.

Some people say, "If the Lord wills, I will do so," when they do not consider the Lord in the matter at all, but simply mean, "If I do not change my mind." Do not throw the odium on the Lord. If you think you may change your mind, do not commit yourself definitely. If you are not fully decided, do not be afraid to say that you do not know what you will do. Be honest enough to let the other know the state of your mind. Be honest in making promises; be honest in fulfilling them.

Fidelity to Promises

Do not make too many promises. He who is too free to promise, places little value upon his promises. He forgets them readily or lets some trifle hinder the performance of them. He always has a ready excuse to ease his conscience and to release himself from the obligation. This indicates a want of character, a lack of real sincerity.

When you make a promise, do not forget it, do not break it. Never disappoint people when you can help it. They feel disappointment as keenly as you do. There is an old saying that "promises are like pie-crust—made to be broken." Are your promises of the pie-crust variety?

Possibly you have heard the story of the old deacon. A man came to him one day to endeavor to get him to fulfil a promise that he had made. The deacon refused. The other urged and entreated him, but still he refused, and finally said, "The Bible says that we should let our words be yea, yea, and nay, nay; and my words are so." "Yes," quickly retorted the other, "when you are asked to make a promise, they are yea, yea; but when you are asked to fulfil it, they are nay, nay." This is one brand of yea-and-nay Christians, but not the kind in whom God delights or man trusts.

When you make promises, keep them. They are a

test of your character. I do not mean that you should be under bondage to your promises. Sometimes we fully believe we can and will perform them, but later find that it is impossible. In such a case we should explain matters and so relieve the mind of the one to whom the promise was made and show him that the failure to make good our word is not due to neglect or unwillingness. Keep your business promises. Many persons get into debt and promise to pay and then just let things drift along. This is wrong. Pay your debts when you agree to, or give a reason for not doing so, and let it be a reason, not an excuse. If you promise to do work for some one, do it. Keep your promise if you must sacrifice to do so.

Many parents are very careless and inconsiderate regarding their promises to their children. Children will "tease" for things if allowed. Too many times parents make promises that they do not expect ever to fulfil, just to be rid of the children's asking. Children soon learn the value of such promises, and they learn the value of your character. Do not lie to your children; do not make promises to them unless you mean them. If you make promises to them and then are not able to keep them, value your word enough and their respect enough to explain to them the reason.

Reader, what is your word worth? What value do you place on it? What value do others place on it? What value does God place on it? God wants you to "speak the truth, and lie not." Your standing, your influence, your usefulness—all depend upon your faithfulness; and if you are faithful, you will be faithful

to your promises. Think seriously over these things.
If you are at fault, set about to amend. Such a fault
will be a blight upon your life and upon your character
until it is corrected. When the Psalmist pictures a
righteous man, he says that he "sweareth [promiseth]
to his own hurt, and changeth not." Are you that sort
of righteous person?

TALK SIXTEEN

HOW TO KEEP OUT OF TROUBLE

Old Uncle John was not so spry as he had once been. There were only a few black hairs left among the many gray ones. His limbs were shaky and his steps faltering. He was "no good for work any more," he said; but there were two things that he kept on doing right along: he seemed to be always smiling and he seemed to be always praising the Lord. "Happy John," people called him, and he certainly deserved the name. He did not seem to have much of this world's goods to make him glad. His lot in life did not appear to be more than usually pleasant, nor was there anything in the way of external evidence to show whence his happiness came. I had often sat and gazed upon his placid face lifted in devotion to God. He never seemed to get into trouble. No matter what happened, Uncle John seemed to have no part in the trouble. With others, troubles came and troubles went, but Uncle John still smiled and praised the Lord.

One day I was standing outside the meeting-house with a little company of brethren, when Uncle John came walking out, smiling as usual and praising the Lord. One of the brethren said to him, "Uncle John, how does it come that you are always so happy and never seem to get into trouble?" He stopped and looked at the speaker with a broad smile, and answered, "I just praise the Lord and mind my own business." He turned and walked away, but his words lingered in my ears and were

indelibly impressed upon my memory. His secret was
very simple, but very effective. And thus he went on
smiling, praising the Lord and minding his own business, and he was "happy John" even to the end. Many
years ago he went to his reward, but the lesson that I
learned that day has never been lost.

Uncle John's rule for keeping out of trouble seemed
very simple. It looks very easy to mind one's own business, but it is one of the hardest things in the world to
do, because it is one of the hardest things in the world
for us to be willing to do. The Scripture says, "Every
fool will be meddling," and it is so hard for some folks
not to act like fools, anyway in this particular respect,
even though they are ever so wise. The affairs of others
are so interesting to them! This is a very human trait,
but it sometimes leads to unpleasant consequences.

God knew the failing of people on this line, so he
said, "Study to be quiet, and to do your own business"
(1 Thess. 4:11). You have, no doubt, studied a great
many lessons, but have you studied this particular one?
It is evident that many have not yet learned this if they
have studied over it. Probably they did not know that
it requires studying. Possibly they never thought of it as
being an object for study. But it is. We shall never
graduate in the school of wisdom until we study this
lesson and learn it thoroughly. "Study to be quiet and
to do your own business." That is the lesson. Have
you learned it? Some folks are always talking, talking,
talking. There seems to be no end to their talk. When
people talk so much they are sure to talk of some things
that should not be talked of. Some people can not keep

an experience of salvation because they talk too much, and as a result they have a great deal of spiritual trouble that might be avoided. But, then, they are so interested in their friends and neighbors! How can they help talking about them? Why, just let them spend their time in studying to be quiet. Let them give themselves a few lessons in minding their own business.

Peter had that human trait. He was interested in what John was going to do. When he asked the Lord, "What shall this man do?" he received an answer. He did not have to wait for it. It was this, "What is that to thee? Follow thou me." I have known many good Christian people who became mixed up in neighborhood or family affairs and got into a great mess of trouble because they failed to mind their own business. If there is a dog-fight going on, all the dogs in the community seem to want to join in it. There seems to be something in humanity that is very much the same. If there is trouble in the community they want to mix into it some way or another. Trouble is a thing that is much easier to get into than it is to get out of.

More people get into trouble through the wrong use of their tongues than through any other means, I suppose. The Wise Man says, "He that keepeth his tongue keepeth his soul from trouble." He also says, "The beginning of strife is as when one letteth out water." You know how it runs in every direction, so that you can not gather it up again nor confine it. Never meddle with the strife of others. You are sure of an abundant crop of trouble if you do. It is written, "He that passeth by and meddleth with strife belonging not to him is

like one that taketh a dog by the ears.'' You know how
that is: if he holds fast he will get into trouble, and if
he lets go he will get into trouble.

There are some people who are religious and who seem
to get along pretty well until their children get mixed up
in trouble with some one. Just as sure as that happens
they are in the trouble, too. They think that their children could not be to blame. They take the children's
part, and trouble is the result. And when they have got-
ten out of the trouble, if they do get out, they have
dishonored both themselves and their religion. There are
others who can never let trouble alone if their friends or
neighbors are in it. They will mix in. They feel that
they must defend their friends, and they are often so
partial in their feelings toward them that they can not
believe them to be in the wrong. They become all heated
in the thing, and before they know it they have a big
case of spiritual trouble on hand in addition to the
other trouble.

When people get into trouble, they like to tell others
about it. If you have sympathetic ears for trouble, you
can hear plenty of it. When you hear such things, it
is very easy to pass them on to some one else. Never let
yourself be a news-carrier for trouble. You will have
trouble of your own if you do. The only business that
a Christian has in relation to such troubles is as a peace-
maker, and even then he must be very cautious and
wise, or he will become involved.

Few people want to take God's way out of trouble.
They will do anything to have their own way out. We
are told to leave off strife before it is meddled with.

That is the only safe way. While you are out, keep out; and the only way to keep out is to mind your own business. Try Uncle John's rule. It will work very well. It is a splendid preventive of trouble. Would you be happy? Would you have the confidence of your neighbors and associates? Would you be free from worldly entanglements? Would you have a contented heart and a cheerful mind? Would you be worthy of the esteem of the people? Would you be different from worldly people? Would you be a sunshine-bearer for your neigh borhood? There is just one way to do it. You must do as "happy John" did—smile, praise the Lord, and mind your own business.

TALK SEVENTEEN

WHAT THE REDBIRD TOLD ME

It was a cold winter morning. Snow covered the ground. The frost on the trees sparkled in the bright sunlight like ten thousand diamonds. But the brightness outside seemed to find no reflection in me. I had been confined to my bed for more than six months. I was gloomy and despondent. It seemed as though all the light and joy had gone out of my life and that only pain and suffering and sorrow were left to me. I had no desire to live. Again and again I prayed that I might die. I should have welcomed any form of death, even the most horrible. I had grown morbid, and almost despaired. I had been prayed for again and again, but the healing touch came not. Life seemed to hold for me no ray of hope, no gleam of sunshine.

As I lay brooding in my melancholy state, a red grosbeak, with his bright red plumage, alighted on a tree a few feet from my window. His eyes sparkled as he gazed at me with interest. He turned his head now this way and now that, apparently studying me intently, and then he gave a cheery call and hopped as near to me as he could get and repeated his cries over and over. Somehow his cries took the form of words in my mind. This is what he said to me: "You, you, you, cheer up, cheer up, cheer up." He hopped about from limb to limb, wiping his beak, picking at pieces of bark, but ever and anon hopping back to look at me and cry again. "Cheer up, cheer up, cheer up." This he did for a long time, then he flew away, only to return soon and to peer at me again, crying his merry "You, you, you, cheer up, cheer up, cheer up." For more than two hours he continued to repeat this and then went away, and far in the distance I heard the last echoes of his notes still saying, "Cheer up, cheer up."

It seemed as though God had sent the bird to bring a message to my soul; and as I thought of the cold and the snow and the winter winds, of the bird's uncertain supply of food, of his many enemies, and considered that, in spite of all this, he could be so cheerful and gay, it made me feel ashamed that I should be so melancholy and despondent. His message, enforced by his example, sank into my heart. I began to think over the favorable side of my situation. I began to consider how many things the Lord had bestowed upon me in the past—his mercy, his kindness, and his blessings. My heart took courage, hope began to lift herself up from the dust. I reflected over the way I had yielded to discouragement. I saw that if I was ever to rise above it I must set myself resolutely to the task of looking upon the bright side and of overcoming the gloom and heaviness. The message of the bird made me ashamed to submit longer to my feelings. I resolved then and there that I would be different. And from that day I began to act and think and speak more cheerfully. Many times I had to act contrary to the way I felt, but I found that this was having an influence upon my feelings, and the more I practised being cheerful the more cheerful I became. Many times I have been sorely pressed down in spirit, but I have found that I can act cheerfully and talk cheerfully even in the midst of depression, and that this is not hypocrisy, but the true way in which to meet such things and conquer them.

Cheerfulness is largely a matter of habit. We must do one of two things—either yield to our feelings and let them be our master or compel our feelings to yield to us that we may be their master. It is a case of conquering or being conquered. So many persons are at the mercy of their emotions. If they do not feel well in body, or their mind is troubled, or their spiritual sky is clouded, they yield themselves to gloomy thoughts and look upon the dark side of the picture. Their thoughts and feelings are reflected in their faces and actions and words. This, in turn, reacts upon them, and they then feel worse in body and mind. Every one around them knows how they feel. This is putting a premium on your bad feelings. It is encouraging them. And it is a very bad habit. You can be cheerful if you will. Do not wear your troubles on your face. Do not let them put a note of sadness in your voice. Cease your sighing: you are only adding to your burdens. Take the bird's advice and cheer up. You can if you will. You can hide your burdens instead of advertising them. To hide them will help you to forget them. You have a place to put your burdens—"Casting all your care upon Him."

I still suffer; I still have periods of mental depression; but I have learned to be cheerful and not let these things be on exhibition. I find it now the easier, and by far the better, way. Cheerfulness is a habit; get the habit. It depends upon you, not upon your circumstances. You can rule your circumstances instead of letting them rule you. Take hold of your bad feelings with a will and conquer them with cheerfulness. The task may not be easy at first, but keep at it and you will win. Do not despair if you lose a few battles. You may have cultivated gloom for so long a time that it has become the fixed state of your mind. Overcome the habit. God will help you. When your feelings become gloomy, say, "I will not be so," and force your mind into other channels. It will want to go back to its former habit, but as often as you catch yourself thinking along gloomy lines turn your thoughts back to the sunshine. Put good cheer into your voice and a smile on your face, no matter how you feel. It will prove a tonic for soul, mind, and body. Listen to the redbird. Hear his merry "Cheer up, cheer up," and act upon his advice. You will find it worth while.

TALK EIGHTEEN

WHAT OLD BILL COULD NOT DO

Old Bill M— was a drunkard. Everybody knew it. People expected to see him stagger as he walked; that was the common thing. As a young man he had been the leader among his chums, and people thought he would make his mark in the world. He had excelled most of his companions, but alas! it was not in the things that make men noble and great. As people said, "The drink was getting him." He was a familiar figure in each of the three saloons in A—. He was popular, for he was good-natured and jolly. He was still the leader of a company, who called themselves the "bunch." Each night they made the rounds of the saloons, then at a late hour staggered homeward.

Yes, Old Bill was a drunkard. He had tried many times to quit. His friends had warned him and advised him to quit. His wife had begged him a hundred times, with tears running down her face. He had promised again and again, had tried, over and over, to master the habit, but it held him fast. One night when he went home, drunk as usual, he found his wife seriously ill. Three days he watched by her bedside, and then the end came. In her dying hour she laid her hand on his and asked him once more for her sake, and his own, to quit drinking. Bill promised with hot tears falling like rain, and he meant it with all his heart.

Two days later he followed her body to the church, and as he took his last look at that still form, he vowed with all his strength of will never to touch drink again. He walked silently back to his home, but it was not home any more. He was heart-broken. What would he do? How could he bear it? Presently two of his comrades came out to sympathize with him. After talking a while, one pulled a bottle from his pocket, saying, "Here, Bill, take a bit to brace you up." "No, Jack," he answered, "I'm going to quit the stuff; I promised her I would." "That's all right," said Jack, "but you need a little now for your nerves." He lifted the bottle to his own lips, then held it uncorked in his hand. The odor entered Bill's nostrils, the old appetite asserted itself, and before he knew it he had seized the bottle. A minute later it was empty! When Bill next came to realize what was happening, it was a week later. He had been drunk all the time; he did not even know what day it was; but when he realized what had happened, he was stricken with remorse. He knew now, as never before, that drink was his master.

Two years passed. His few belongings had been sold to pay the funeral expenses; the remainder had gone for drink. Another family lived in the home now. Mr. Wilson, a kind neighbor, had given him a home, and he worked for him when he was sober enough. One evening as he was making his way to the saloon as usual, he heard singing. "That's strange," he muttered; "wonder what's going on?" He turned and walked toward the singing and soon found a large tent filled with people. "Queer-looking show," he thought as he approached the entrance. A pleasant-faced young man stepped up to him and said, "Come in, Bill, and I will get you a

good seat." He mechanically followed the usher in.
The singing was good, and he enjoyed it. Presently a
man arose and, with tears running down his face, re-
lated that he had been a drunkard, and that after years
of trying to overcome the habit, he had finally turned to
God for help, and that he was now a free and happy
man. Bill understood the struggle part, but not the
rest. He knew what it meant to fail, and as he pondered
he thought of his wife. Did she know how he had broken
his promise? Did she weep over him now as she used to?

Some one entered the pulpit and talked for a long
time, but Bill did not hear anything he said. Bill was
thinking, thinking. There was a man who had "beat
the drink," and he said the Lord had helped him. Bill
wondered if the Lord would help him. When the preacher finished, the first man rose again; Bill straightened
up and looked keenly. "Yes," he thought, "he has been
a drinker all right, and a hard one; his face shows it."
The speaker was inviting men to Christ for the help they
needed.

Old Bill never quite knew how it happened, but he
suddenly found himself up in front holding the stranger's hand and telling him that he wanted help to quit
drink. Side by side they knelt while the saved man
earnestly poured out his heart to God for the drunkard.
Old Bill did not know how to pray, he had never tried
in his life, but he wanted help; all his soul longed for it.
He listened to the other man praying. He was asking
for just what Bill needed; his heart joined in. Yes, he
wanted to quit drinking; he wanted to be a good man,
but he had to have help. The other man prayed as

though God were right close by, and Bill felt that He must be, so he said: "Yes, God, I'll quit it if you'll help me. I'll be a man if you'll help me, but I can't do it by myself!" That was all, but he meant it, and he felt that God would help him. A strange, quiet peace came into his heart, and he really felt happy. He went home sober that night.

Some of the "bunch" outside the tent had seen Bill go forward, and soon the news was in all the saloons. "He'll be back by Saturday night," they said. But he did not come back. Instead he was in the meeting telling the people what wonderful things God had done for him. He did not want strong drink any more at all, he declared. The "bunch" did not believe this. They laughed and made many prophecies; they waited week by week, but Old Bill came to the saloon no more. Two years passed; Bill lived a joyful Christian life and never tired of telling what the Lord had done for him. He went out to a country schoolhouse, where he organized a Sunday-school and labored zealously and successfully.

There were many temptations. At first the "bunch" laughed and made him the butt of many rude jests, then they laid plans to trap him. One day one of them stuck an open whisky-bottle under his nose, saying, "Smell it, Bill; ain't it a fine odor?" Bill stepped back, all smiles, and said quietly, "Well, Tom, drink was my master a long time, but I have a better Master now." He went on his way unobstrusively but steadily, and finally won the respect and confidence of all.

At last the end came; Old Bill was dead. There was a peaceful smile upon his face, for his sun had gone down in splendor. The "bunch" followed him to the grave. They could not quite understand even yet what had happened to him. It was a wonderful change, and his life had won their respect, and they followed him silently to his last resting-place. After the burial they stood talking it over in a little group by themselves. "I thought the drink had him sure," said one; "I don't see how he beat it." "It was not Bill who did it," said a quiet voice behind them; "it was Jesus Christ." They turned and saw the pastor walking away. "Guess the parson must have it right," said one of them. "It was a pretty good job, too."

TALK NINETEEN

DIVINE AND WORLDLY CONFORMITY

The Scriptures say, "Be not conformed to this world: but be ye transformed by the renewing of your mind" (Rom. 12:2). They also say that we should be "conformed to the image of his Son" (Rom. 8:29). We have here two sorts of conformity, one of which is condemned and the other approved. Much is said by some classes of religious professors about worldly conformity, while little is said about divine conformity. It is my purpose herein to point out the essential nature of these two kinds of conformity.

By worldly conformity most religious teachers mean outward likeness of dress, manner, customs, etc. This, however, is not its true significance. Conformity to Christ does not mean dressing as he dressed, speaking the language that he spoke, eating the same kind of food that he ate, or observing any of those externals that went to make up his life.

In the true meaning of the word, conformity goes deeper than externals. Two things may look very much alike and yet be very different in their natures. Pyrites of iron looks so much like gold that it has deceived many a person into thinking that he had found riches. For this reason it is called "fool's gold." Likewise things may outwardly seem very different, while in reality they are very much the same. A sparkling diamond seems very different from a lump of coal, but the chief difference is only in the arrangement of their particles. Both are composed chiefly of carbon, so in nature they conform closely to each other.

Conformity is a thing of nature, not of external appearance. We are "by nature the children of wrath." Our likeness to the world consists in a likeness of character, and for that reason we are told that we must be transformed. This transformation is a change of character; it has to do, first of all, with internals, not with externals.

Conformity to the world in most externals is not only advisable but necessary. We wear clothing as the world does; we live in houses built like those around us; we speak the same language as sinners; we have the same habits of thought and speech in general that they have; we use the same implements and tools; we raise the same crops; we employ the same methods of work and business; in fact, we conform to the world in all these things. We can not avoid doing this without sacrificing what is vital and proper in our lives. Conformity to the world in these externals becomes evil only when such conformity has its origin in an evil principle in the heart or when it produces an evil effect.

When Christ prayed for his disciples, he said, "Keep them from the evil." Paul said, "As using and not abusing." It is that which is evil, or the evil use that is made of externals, that is obnoxious to God. A proper use of all things is permissible, and if our hearts are conformed to God, we naturally desire and seek only the proper use of things. But the natural heart is wicked; it is set on pleasing itself; it is full of vanity and pride.

So long as this condition exists, the heart is not conformed to God. There must be a transformation, and this is not one which starts from the outside and works inward, for such at best could be only a reformation. The real transformation is a thing that begins on the inside and works a vital change in the spiritual condition and character. When this internal change is wrought, it gives a new quality and direction to the whole range of thought and activity. It manifests itself in new desires and aspirations, in new habits and customs, in newness of speech and looks and behavior. When we are transformed so that we become new creatures in Christ Jesus, we begin to act like new creatures. But our bodies are not transformed: we still have bodies of flesh, which retain their natural desires and appetites, and these we may gratify in a lawful way without sin.

When the heart is transformed and purified from its vanity and pride, these qualities will not be manifested in external things. But so long as pride and vanity remain in the heart, preaching to people and requiring them to cease wearing worldly adornment is like trying to kill a tree by pulling off some of its leaves—the people may lay off such things under pressure, but they are no better than before. People must be taught the Bible standard of externals, but the chief thing is to get their hearts right. When the heart is conformed to the image of Christ, the words of the old song are true of it:

> "There's no thirsting for life's pleasure,
> Nor adorning rich and gay;
> For I've found a richer treasure,
> One that fadeth not away."

Neither force nor persuasion is required to get persons with such an experience to act properly regarding external things.

In carrying out their idea of non-conformity to the world, some bodies of people have adopted a special garb or a special form of speech to distinguish them from others. This, however, is not a mark of real non-conformity, but a mark of sectarianism. The true and only difference needful between ourselves and the world in externals is that we are to reject those things that are evil or that produce evil. All things else are lawful to us, though these lawful things must also be judged by the law of expediency.

Conformity to Christ means conformity in character. It means purity of desire, so that our hearts reach out for only those things that are pure, and we are moved by pure motives and actuated by holy purposes. It means that we have a conscience toward God in whatever we do. It means to put his will before everything else. It means that the dominating purpose of our life will be to please him in every detail, and not ourselves. A heart like this is not attracted by the vain and sinful things of the world; on the contrary, it is repelled by them.

When the person is adorned with gold, jewels, costly or gaudy array, or immodest clothing, we must needs look for the root in the heart. There is where the trouble lies. There is the seat of the desire. It is useless to take off the externals while the internal corruption is permitted to continue. God hates all vanity and pride. There is no such element in his character. If we are conformed to him, there is no such element in our character; and if our character is purged from these things, we have no desire for their external manifestations. God loves meekness and modesty, and these are the opposites of display. If we are meek and modest in character, our dress and deportment will manifest these qualities. If we do not manifest them, it is because we do not possess them.

It may not be out of place here to call attention to the Bible principles relating to the subject of dress and personal adornment. In beginning this phase of the subject we should note that the gospel is not a set of rules, but a revelation of moral principles. It is intended for all people in all countries, climates, and ages. We should not, therefore, expect that these principles as they relate to dress would be revealed in other than the most general terms, or applied to the details of the subject. There is just one principle involved; we may sum up the whole subject under that one heading. The Bible standard of dress consists of just three words, but these three words cover the whole scope of life. They are, "in modest apparel" (1 Tim. 2:9). This is the standard, and this is the whole standard. We are given a hint regarding how to apply this standard, but our own good judgment is sufficient to draw the line in the right place, provided our hearts are conformed to the divine image. There is no excuse for fanaticism any more than there is for pride. Sound judgment and good sense will help us avoid both extremes.

A definition of modesty is, "Restrained within due limits of propriety; free from indecency or lewdness;

not excessive or extreme; moderate.'' A Christian's apparel should be modest in cut, that is, in the way it is made; it should cover the body as a modest person would cover it, not displaying those parts that the prevailing standards of modesty require to be covered. Judged by this standard, very many religious professors come far short, their clothing being less than decency really requires. Such a thing, of course, does not have its origin in a pure heart. The woman who displays herself to attract attention is anything but modest.

· Clothing should be made to conform to modesty in all other respects also. Useless things added to one's apparel for the purpose of display and show do not conform to modesty. ''Loud'' and flashy colors are not modest. The Bible does not forbid us to wear any particular shade, but there are shades and combinations that are showy and gaudy, and by their extremeness violate modesty, for modesty is the avoidance of extreme. Whatever we wear, it should be modest in color just as well as in other particulars.

Christian apparel should be modest in texture; that is, it should not be so thin that it displays the body or the underwear. No man thinks a woman modest who wears goods so thin as to display her under-garments, or hosiery so thin as to display her limbs. Such things are very unbecoming to saints, and of course not less so to other people. Sisters, dress so that a modest man will not feel embarrassed in your presence.

Apparel should be modest as to cost. It should not be what the Scriptures term ''costly array.'' It is well to buy good material, and for such we must pay a good price, but this is not what the Bible means by "costly array." It means not to be extravagant. We should not waste money, but make the best possible use of it.

Some have thought it wrong to try to make our clothes becoming. This is not the case. The Bible says "that women *adorn* themselves in modest apparel"; that is, their apparel should be such as adorns or becomes them, so long as it is modest clothing. It should be adapted in cut, color, etc., to harmonize with the complexion, size, and height of the person. We owe it to ourselves to make a good appearance. To make ourselves outlandish or conspicuous in any way is neither wise nor right. It is violating modesty, and this is not consistent. It is only when we make a proper appearance that we can have a proper influence, and so be effective for God.

God delights in modesty in dress, in words, in actions —in all things. Pride and show are an abomination to him, and if we conform to him in our inner life and character, outward conformity will naturally follow; but if inward desire runs out after that which is immodest and gaudy, if the heart desires to display upon the person gold and jewels and finery, it is because it does not conform to the image of God's Son, but to the world.

TALK TWENTY

BAPTIZED WITH FIRE

John the Baptist said, when speaking of the work of the coming Messiah, "He shall baptize you with the Holy Ghost and with fire." The symbolic tongues of fire which sat on the believers on the day of Pentecost represented a very real something which from henceforth would be manifested in their lives. It is not my purpose here to enter into an explanation of the Baptist's words. I wish to speak only of the fervency which fire represents as it should characterize our lives. The life that has in it no fervency has little or nothing of God. The soul that is vigorous in God is a soul full of power. We need to be "on fire" for God, and there are three ways in which this fervency should manifest itself.

A Burning Love

We need a fervent love. It is the foundation, as it were, of all Christian fervency. If our love lacks fervency, it lacks the vital element that makes it effective. If our love for God is kindled into a burning passion, it will put him before all else. His will and desire will be the delight of our hearts. His service will be no task, to sacrifice for him will be easy, and to obey him will be our meat. It will make our consciences tender toward him. What he loves we shall love, and whom he loves we shall love. If our love is fervent, we shall love truth, and we shall love it as it is worthy to be loved— above our own opinions or ideas and more than the teachings of men. We will not sacrifice it or deny it for ease or comfort or to please others. We shall strive to make our lives conform to it. We shall labor with all our strength to spread it over the world. If we love the truth, we shall be missionaries whether we are at home or abroad. Love begets labor.

A fervent love of the brethren glows in the heart that is full of God. It will burn up criticism and backbiting. It will burn up division and strife. It will destroy jealousy and envy. It will make peace in the home, in the church, and in the individual heart. A thousand troubles come when love grows cold: the eyes see no more as they once saw, the ears hear no more as before, the tongue talks differently, and the heart feels differently, the glow dies out of the eyes, the tenderness leaves the touch, sympathy wanes in the heart, and there is ashes for beauty and heaviness instead of praise. When the first love is left, when the divine fire is quenched, out of the life has gone its richness, its transfiguring beauty; and what is left?

O brother, sister, keep the red glow of fervency in your love. If you have lost it, rest not till it is rekindled. Love makes us strong to do and to bear. John Knox said to God, "Give me Scotland or I die." That was love that shook a kingdom. Paul counted not his life dear to him. That was love that overthrew the idols of the heathen. God "so loved the world," and a new era dawned, bringing light and salvation. If we have such love, it will work out in effectual action. A church fervent in love is a church reaching out and winning others. It is a church with an all-absorbing passion for the lost. Let us ask ourselves today, ''Have I a fervent love? or am I cold and has my love lost its strength?''

A Burning Zeal

A man or a church without zeal is of necessity ineffective. What is the temperature of your zeal? Does it let you go for months without speaking to a soul about his salvation? Does it permit you to rest easy while others are toiling, praying, and sacrificing? About how much time on an average do you spend each day praying for souls, or for the progress of the kingdom of God in the earth? About how often do you pray definitely for some of your neighbors, your friends, or business associates? About how long has it been since you invited some one to Christ? When did you pray with some one for his spiritual needs? When did you speak encouraging words? When did you give some one a tract or paper? When did you write a letter filled with spiritual advice or help? How much sacrifice are you making for the cause? How much time, labor, or money have you expended for the kingdom in the past year? Is your zeal dead, or is it in fervent activity? How much does the salvation of the world mean to you?

Behold the zeal of the advocates of some of the false movements of these days! See how they pour out their money like water. See how they never can be satisfied unless they are laboring for their movement. Are we as zealous as they? If not, why not? If we have the truth and know that we have it, should not that be enough to fire our zeal till it would not let us rest while there are others in darkness? Almost in sight of you, or perhaps within a stone's throw, are people who do not know the truth. If you do no more than you have done the past year, may they not live and die there and never know it?

Zeal does not ask for excuses. Zeal is never satisfied till it has gone full length in labor. When one man was asked what was the secret of the marvelous success of the early church in its fight against heathenism, he replied with just one word, "Zeal." The same sort of zeal will produce results today. Zeal must, of course, be enlightened. It can succeed only when guided by wisdom. Blind zeal is like a blind horse: it is likely to run in any direction regardless of results. So be wise when you are zealous. If you are truly wise with that wisdom "which cometh down from above," you will also be zealous.

A Fervent Hatred

A good Christian is a good hater. "Ye that love the Lord hate evil." This is an age of toleration. Almost any false doctrine may be preached, while many of the religious teachers of so-called orthodoxy plod on their way indifferently. Error thrives, a multitude of souls are deceived, but many seem but little concerned. Evil raises its head everywhere and sneers at the Christian people. Dens of vice, gambling-houses, lewd picture-shows, and a hundred other forms of evil are tolerated and even looked upon as "necessary evils" by religious professors. He who really loves God just as truly hates all evil. He so hates it in himself that he will give it no place in his heart or life. He hates it in others. He sees no pleasant thing in it. To him it is foul, vile, and revolting. It is his enemy, and he is its bitter foe. The measure of his love for good is the measure of his hatred for evil. We can not love the good more than we hate the evil. The two exactly balance in our lives.

A burning love, a burning zeal, and a burning hatred will make your life as a beacon-light to the world; and if you would be a true example of what God means men to be, you must have this fervency in your life. It alone can keep you from coldness. It alone can make you a prosperous, victorious Christian.

TALK TWENTY-ONE

WHAT TO DO WITH THE DEVIL

Some people say there is no devil, but I am convinced that he is very real. In fact, I have had some personal experiences with him that leave no room for doubt. He is right here in this world. Like a lion he ''goeth about seeking whom he may devour.'' What to do with him is the biggest problem that faces some Christians. They spend so much time thinking about the devil, fearing him, and trying to combat him, that they have little time for God. Their testimony is a testimony of the devil's doings and their conflict with him. Their religion is a negative, not a positive, thing. It consists in *not* doing and *not* being, *not* thinking and *not* feeling or in trying not to. They are working on the problem from the wrong end. Our problem is to do and be, to live a positive life. Life is for accomplishment and for char-acter-building. The overcoming of the obstacles that we meet is only incidental; it is not the main purpose of our lives. A great many persons think that they could accomplish great things and be wonderful Christians if it were not for the devil. What to do with him is their problem. I shall tell you what to do.

First, do not be afraid of him. Have you not read these words, ''Greater is he that is in you, than he that is in the world''? If you will just believe that, you will have no cause to fear the devil. Do you not know that God is in you? and if he is in you, is he not more than a match for your adversary? "If God be for us, who can be against us?" Satan may oppose us, but he can not prevail against us. His opposition and his schemes will be brought to naught. Just add a little boldness to faith, and you will overcome him. Do not be frightened at his roaring. He can not touch you unless God permits, and if God permits him, it will only be to give you the greater victory in the end. Are you God's child? Will he permit anything that will do you permanent ill? Do not fear the devil; trust God. Give your attention and strength to pleasing him. If you will keep busy doing this, you will not have so much trouble with Satan. God does not want you to be shivering with fear. He wants you to "be strong in the Lord and in the power of his might."

Satan is like a lion; but when a lion roared against Samson, that man slew the beast with his naked hands because the Spirit of the Lord was upon him. If, instead of fearing, you will trust in the Lord to put his Spirit upon you when there is need of it, you may overcome Satan as easily as Samson did the lion. Daniel was thrown into the lions' den, but they did not eat him. God put a muzzle on them, not a literal muzzle, but something still more effectual, and they could not touch Daniel.

Being afraid of the devil is much like being afraid of the darkness. When I was a boy, I was bold enough to go where I wanted to in the darkness; but when I started for the house again, I could imagine that dogs and bears and all sorts of frightful things might be anywhere about, so I would run at full speed. There might have been something, but if so, I never really knew it; but I would get panic-stricken just the same. If you become frightened this way in spiritual things, you may look upon it as only a childish habit. You will never be a "really and truly" grown-up man or woman for God until you get over your foolish fear of the devil. We are told to "resist him stedfast in the faith." It is faith that counts. If you have a gun, a crow will not fly near you. If you have faith, the devil will be more afraid of you than you are of him. Try using this weapon on him. You will find it very effectual.

Second, do not run from him. A man from the East was once riding over a Western prairie with a party of friends, when he saw an Indian walking along. While he was looking at the Indian, an angry bull, which had been bellowing and pawing up the ground, suddenly charged the Indian. Instead of his running, as the Easterner expected him to do, he simply turned about, folded his arms, stood stock-still, and faced the angry animal. It came charging down till it was almost upon him, then suddenly stopped, looked at him, and ran around him. The Indian stood motionless. The animal bellowed and pawed and ran round and round him. He did not move, and the animal did not touch him, but presently went off and left him alone, after which the Indian went on his way as though nothing had happened. There is a good lesson in that for us. There is no use to run from the devil, for he can run faster than we can. Our victory is often won by our standing still to see the salvation of God.

Third, watch. That is what our Lord commanded,

but he did not say, "Watch the devil." The thing
that we need to watch most is where our own feet are
going. If we allow ourselves to be occupied in watching
Satan, we may get out of the path and not know it. The
Bible also says, "looking unto Jesus," not, "looking
unto Satan." It is from God that our help comes. When
we look at Satan, he appears great and terrible. When
we look to God, we see his greatness and realize how
much greater he is than Satan, and our courage rises,
our strength is increased, our fears vanish, and we become confident. Look to God and where your own feet
are going, and let God manage the devil.

Fourth, ignore him. There is nothing Satan hates so
much as to be ignored. For us to calmly go upon our
way unafraid and trustful, not dismayed by his roaring,
is not at all to his liking. If we will keep our hearts
and minds occupied with good things and pay no attention to his threats, we shall find that he will go off
and leave us. He may soon return, but if you meet him
in the same way, he will not linger around you as he
will if he can hold your attention upon himself.

You have better use for your time than to let the
enemy occupy it. Use it in active service for God. Jesus said he would give us "rest unto our souls." Do
you have that rest? God means for you to have it, but
you can not have it if you keep your attention on Satan
all the time. He will tantalize you if you will let him.
While you are looking unto Jesus, you will not see the
faces that Satan makes at you, and so will not be troubled. If you will listen to God, you will not have time
to listen to Satan. If he is constantly troubling you,

it is because you are giving him opportunity. He is a conquered foe. The victory is yours, if you will have it so.

TALK TWENTY-TWO

WAITING ON THE LORD

Some people are always in a hurry about things. If
they want to do something or to have something, they
can not wait, they must do it or have it at once. When
they are compelled to wait, the time seems very long
and their impatience grows with every delay. They
can not quietly and patiently wait for anything.

Such persons bring this same characteristic into their
spiritual lives. When they pray, they want an immediate answer—they want God to hurry up. If the answer
is delayed, they get all worked up about it. Sometimes
they murmur against the Lord and feel very bad, like
spoiled children. Sometimes they pray a few times for
what they desire, and if the answer does not come they
conclude that God does not mean to answer them; so
they give up seeking for it and sometimes question God's
faithfulness. If they see something that needs doing or
something that is not going to please them, it must be
remedied immediately; if it is not, they are much displeased. They can not wait for a propitious time or
till things have worked out so that they can be properly
handled. Their motto seems to be, "Do it now." That
is all very well for some things, but quite frequently
it is necessary to patiently wait on the Lord and upon
others. We can not hurry the Lord; all time is his.
He works according to his own purposes and will, according to his own wisdom and plans. We can not

choose for him; we must be willing for him to choose
for us. It must be his to say both as to "when" and
"how." Ours is to wait and trust, his to choose and do.

Many years ago I read a story. Later, when I was
lying on my bed of affliction and praying earnestly for
God to restore my health, he brought to my mind this
story and applied its lesson to my soul. It was such
a help to me that I will give it to you also. I had been
much troubled because I was not healed. I would pray
very earnestly, with a longing that seemed to draw out
all my soul. Others would pray also, but there was no
answer from God. Disappointment and discouragement
seemed to shut me in with walls of darkness. A feeling
of helplessness and almost of utter hopelessness came
over me. I was in this condition when God brought to
my memory this long-forgotten story and applied it to
my heart with a peculiar emphasis that made it a direct
message from him to my soul.

This is the story: The king of a certain country was
growing old, and he had no son to succeed him. He
announced to his people that he would choose an heir
to the throne from among the young men of the country
by a competitive test which would give all an equal
chance. On the day appointed a great number of young
men presented themselves. A certain test was made,
and some failed while others passed. Then other tests
came, and each time some were rejected till at last only
three were left.

They were put through test after test, but all seemed
equally able to meet them, so the king announced through
his heralds that on the next day the matter would be

decided by a foot-race. The course was marked off, the judges were at their places, and all was ready. Just at this time a man came up to each of the contestants and said secretly to him, "The king is taking special note of you. Do not run when the signal is given until the king gives you a special signal." The three took their places eager for the race. The signal was given, one bounded forward quickly, then hesitated and stopped; then another sprang forward after him, upon which the first started forward again and they ran for the goal with all speed. The third stood looking anx- iously at the king and at the two runners, murmuring to himself, "I can make it yet, I can make it yet." The king gazed at the runners and gave no heed to the one still standing. The waiting man thought himself forgotten and soon realized that it would be impossible for him to win the race. He felt that all was lost for him.

The two runners ran on at top speed, reaching the goal together. They were brought back, and all three stood before the king. To the first he said, "Were you not told not to run until I gave you the signal? Why then did you run?"

"I forgot," said the man.

Of the second he asked the same question. His re- ply was, "I thought it would be but a moment till you would give the signal, and seeing the other running I ran also."

To the third he said, "And why did not you run?"

"Because you did not give me the signal, sir," he an- swered.

"My son," said the king, "I knew that you could run, but I did not know that you could wait."

So the young man found that the test was not a test of doing but of waiting. And thus the Lord said to me that day, "I knew that you could run, I knew that you would work with all your strength; but can you wait on me?" These words have been repeated over and over in my heart during the long years. It was a hard lesson to learn, and many times I have grown weary, many times I have longed for the end of the waiting; but that lesson has helped me to bear and to wait and to be patient in the waiting. Sometimes it has seemed that the answer would never come. Sometimes it has seemed that the Lord had forgotten. Many times I have had to say to my heart, "Be patient and wait." This is the hardest lesson that many of us ever have to learn, but learn it we must if God's will and his plan are to be fulfilled in our lives.

There are some things for which we do not need to wait, but for which we need to press our petitions with earnestness and diligence and with an out-reaching grasp of faith for a "now" answer—for example, the supplying of a soul-need, such as forgiveness or sanctification, or physical or other help where the need is urgent. Sometimes people think that it is not the Lord's time to save or sanctify them or to give them something else that is needed at once, when the trouble is they do not get in earnest enough or do not exercise faith as they might. God's time for necessary things, and especially for salvation work, is *now;* and if we do not receive when we seek, we may look for the fault in ourselves or in our manner of seeking. Waiting on the Lord is not needful in this class of things and it will only hinder receiving. There are, however, many other things for which we may not know God's time and in the case of which growing impatient and trying to force matters will grieve God and hinder us. Unfulfilled desire patiently and submissively met is often a powerful factor in character-building.

Have you prayed for things, yearned for them, reached out after them, and yet your prayer is not yet answered? Have you been tempted to believe that it was of no use to seek for them? If you are not seeking selfishly, or if God has not denied you, do not lose faith. God has said, "Ask, and ye shall receive"; and again he says, "They shall not be ashamed that wait for me" (Isa. 49:23). God is faithful. He knows what is best. As a loving Father he watches over you. His ear is open to your cry. We are told to "rest in the Lord, and wait patiently for him." Do not grow impatient, do not become wrought up, but while you must wait on the Lord, rest in him. Jeremiah tells us how to wait for God to deliver—"It is good that a man should both hope and quietly wait for the salvation of the Lord" (Lam. 3:26). Think of that expression, "hope and quietly wait." Do not these words mean confidence and soul-rest? Do they not mean assurance and trust? They do not mean, however, that we should be careless. They imply activity of faith and desire, but they shut out fear and unbelief. The Psalmist says, "Wait on the Lord: be of good courage, and he shall strengthen thine heart" (Psa. 27:14). Keep up your courage while you wait, do not grow despondent, be strong in faith; God will not fail.

Again, we are exhorted to "wait on the Lord, and keep his way" (Psa. 37:34). If wrongs are not righted, if persecutions continue, if, like Paul, we have a "thorn in the flesh" and our desires are not granted, let us do what this text tells us—let us "keep His way." Let us serve the Lord just as truly as though conditions were ideal and all our desires satisfied. Let us show our fidelity to God, by being true whether circumstances are favorable or unfavorable. God promised Abraham the land of Canaan, but he went up and down in it for many years as a stranger. His posterity went into Egypt and there, under the lash of the taskmaster, they waited, waited, waited. Did not they have God's promise? Had he not said that that goodly land should be theirs? Why did he wait so long? Was this the way that he fulfilled his promise? Had he forgotten them? Did their cries to him fall on deaf ears? Their waiting was not easy. It was long and oh, how wearisome! Why did God wait so long, was there any adequate reason? Yes, when God waits there is always a good reason for the waiting. His acts are not arbitrary; he does not act according to caprice; he acts wisely and when it is best. He tells us why he delayed in this case · it was because the sins of the Canaanites had not yet come to the full. When they reached that point, the Lord fulfilled his promise and led the children of Israel out of their bondage into that goodly land.

Have you learned this lesson of waiting upon the Lord? Can you commit your ways to him and feel that if desire is still unsatisfied, if obstacles are not yet removed, if trials yet bear upon you, the Father-love is not growing cold, nor his hearing dull, nor has he forgotten? In the proper time and way the answer will be sure, and because of the delay the answer will be fuller and will enrich you more than if it had come when first you asked. Wait patiently on the Lord, trust also in him, be not weary in well-doing, and out of your waiting will come strength, and out of your sorrow will come rejoicing, and out of the bitterness will come sweetness, and at the end of the way you will find a crown and life everlasting.

TALK TWENTY-THREE

THREE NECESSARY "RATIONS"

The soul, like the body, must have something to nourish and strengthen it, to give it vigor and vitality. An army will have neither the strength nor the courage to fight unless it has its rations. And if I may be allowed a play on words, I may say that there are three rations which are very needful to every Christian. Without these he must be weak and faltering and of little service, but with them he may be a pillar of strength in the temple of God.

The first of these "rations" is *aspiration*, or ardent desire. Strong desire is one of the greatest incentives of life. To be contented as we are is one of the most fatal hindrances to progress and activity. There is nothing to stir us to action when desire is satisfied. The trouble with a great multitude of people is that they are satisfied when conditions do not warrant it. If we are to make progress in the Christian life or accomplish anything for God, we must have strong aspirations. These are as a spur to our energies. Aspiration is the cure for being "at ease in Zion." Aspirations are good or bad according to the motive that prompts them. Some are essentially selfish, and such are necessarily evil. If we desire to be or do for selfish advantage, for glory and praise; if we aspire to be leaders, as so many religious people do, only that they may have authority or honor—our aspirations are evil. But each one of us owes it to himself and to God to desire strongly to be and to do his best for God.

What is the temperature of your spiritual aspirations today? Are you so well satisfied that desire is cold and almost lifeless? or are you reaching out to the things that are before with an eager yearning? No matter how good or how holy you may be, if you look Christ-ward until you see the depths of his submission to the Father, the length of his love for souls, the heights of his lofty purity and unworldliness, the tenderness of his sympathy, the richness of his communion with the Father, his self-abnegation, his humility, and his un-swerving faithfulness, your soul will feel itself so im-measurably beneath Christ that you can not help longing to be more like him. It will create in your soul an in-expressible aspiration to draw further away from this old world with its trifles and its follies and to draw nearer to Christ, to be more like him in your inner life, and to act more like him in your outward life. If you look only at self and self-interest, your spiritual aspira-tions will fade away; but as you look away from self and behold Him who is altogether lovely, the more you look upon him the greater will be your desire to be conformed to his likeness and submitted to his will.

Each of us ought to desire to be our best for God. Do not be content to be one of the "weak ones," or even an average Christian. Those souls who rise above the average, those who are bright lights in their communi-ties, are not the ones who are easily satisfied with their attainments, nor are they the ones who are willing to be this year as they were last year or the year before.

You, as well as any one else, can be a bright light if you will. You can be spiritual if you will. It is not a question of God's blessing some more than others; it is a question of desire that spurs to active effort to become spiritual.

There is much work to be done, and you have a part in that work. How great that part may be depends more upon your desire to work than upon anything else. Are you, like many professed Christians, willing enough for others to work and willing to be idle yourself? If you really *want* to do something for the kingdom, there is something that you can do. If you are willing to do anything, no matter what, God will see that you have something to do. No matter how small your task is, it is worth doing well. Look upon the fields, not those afar off, but those about you. All around you are souls going to destruction. Forget your own concern. Look at the needs about you till your heart is filled with desire for these souls, till you covet them for the Master as a miser covets gold. Then you will find work enough to do and strength to do it.

The second "ration" is *inspiration*. There is so much half-hearted work, so much done mechanically, so much form in worship and service. What we need is enthusiasm. We hear much about artistic inspiration and poetic inspiration, but what we really need most of all is spiritual inspiration. Religious forms are cold and dead until there is put into them the warmth of enthusiasm. Get your soul filled with this glowing warmth. It will lighten your tasks. It will bring success instead of failure. It will be a well-spring of joy. It will make an optimist of you. It will help you break down barriers. It will enable you to surmount obstacles. It will put the shout of victory in your soul in the very face of your foes. An enthusiastic man is a victorious man. An enthusiastic church is a victorious church. Enthusiastic work and worship are filled with a vitality that makes them worth while.

Do not be content to be a formalist. Throw yourself into your work. Go at things as though you meant business. Do not be a lazy Christian. An indolent way of doing things can be neither joyful nor successful. The more of your heart you put into your work, the more it will mean to you, and the more it means to you, the more you can accomplish. Have confidence that you will succeed, for confidence will help you attain to your desires. Your energy wisely directed has in it the very element of success. Look at what others are accomplishing by hard work and perseverance. The same qualities in you will win. But keep this one thing in view, that without inspiration or enthusiasm you lack much of the winning quality. Cultivate enthusiasm. Do with your might what your hands find to do.

The third "ration" needful is *consideration*. This serves as a balance for the two former rations. Its absence has caused disaster many times. Many people grow very enthusiastic and aspire to great things, but because they lack consideration they run into wild fanaticism and go to great extremes; and as a result both they and their religion lose the respect and confidence of the people. How especially true this is in some of the modern holiness movements! Their adherents give themselves over to unseemly demonstrations, ignore good judgment, and teach things and do things they would not if they stopped to carefully consider them.

Salvation and all that pertains to it stand on the foundation of wisdom and good sense. Anything that is not according to these is out of harmony with the true principles of religion. So we should weigh our every act and all our teachings in the balance of good judgment. What in our lives or teaching does not appeal to the sound judgment and good sense of others had better be rejected. Genuine holiness, because of its reasonableness, appeals to the intellect and heart of every man. Extremism and fanaticism are not part of true religion. Throw plenty of enthusiasm into your work, but see to it that that enthusiasm is held in proper channels by consideration. Do not let it overflow without bounds. It is sure to run in the wrong direction if you do.

God has given us the power of consideration and understanding to control and guide our energies. By means of these faculties we get the highest and best use of our powers. To act without consideration is very often to act wrongly. God's acts are always wise, and to be godlike means for us to use what wisdom he gives to us.

Let us be sure that we have these three needful "rations" and that we make the use of them that God has designed. We shall then be successful Christians and accomplish the work that it pleases God for us to do. Aspire to be and do your best. Throw your soul into whatever you undertake. Be careful and considerate in all your ways, so that you "shall neither be barren nor unfruitful," but that you "shall be like a tree planted by the rivers of water, that bringeth forth his fruit in his season."

TALK TWENTY-FOUR

A RETREAT, OR A ROUT?

Armies often suffer defeat, but there is a great difference in the way they take defeat. Sometimes an army is overcome and driven out of its position, but retreats only as far as it must, then turns again upon the foe to courageously renew the conflict. Other armies have been defeated, and in a panic have thrown away their weapons and fled in disorder. The first, though defeated, retains its honor, while the others have nothing but shame.

Similar things are seen in individual lives. There are those who suffer temporary defeat, but who count it only temporary and set themselves immediately to the task of gathering together their forces and retrieving what they have lost. Others, when they realize a defeat, give up all as lost, throw down their weapons, and cease to fight. They forsake the ranks of God's people, sometimes for a very trifling reason, and go back into the world and suffer the shame that attaches to a backslider. The serious part of this is that many can do such a thing and consider it a rather light matter. Instead of being a light matter, turning away from God is one of the most terrible things that a soul can do and one which is often fraught with the direst results and would be every time were it not for the exceeding mercy of God. How it is that one who has ever truly loved God can turn away from him and plunge again into the follies of the world, doing those things which he knows God abhors, is more than I can understand. Sometimes those who once seemed to be quite spiritual are now among the most wicked, even worse than before they ever made a profession.

In one of the Southern States lived a lady who had at different times professed to be saved, but as often backslid. Her daughter, while conversing with me one day, said, "When Mother goes back, she goes full length to the world." She went on to tell me that when her mother gave up her profession she at once laid aside her plain attire and decked herself in jewelry and gay clothing and began attending worldly places of amusement. She seemed to think that when she no longer claimed to be saved she could cast off all restraint and ignore God's claims upon her entirely, and that it did not matter what she did now. Her excuse was, "Oh, I am not saved now." Just as though that changed in any degree her solemn responsibility to obey God!

I was talking with a man who had been a preacher. I spoke to him about something that had happened in his life on a certain occasion. He had been guilty of immoral conduct. He acknowledged it with apparently no sense of shame, saying, "Oh, I was not professing then." He acted as though he thought his past conduct made no difference in respect to his present standing or influence. Some people seem to think that backsliding gives them some sort of indulgence or license to act as they please. Such a view is equally dishonoring to God and to themselves. Sin makes a stain that never can be eradicated. Do not forget this. I make the statement advisedly. I am aware that many persons do not view it thus, but it is only because they do not consider the question as it should be considered. Even the blood of Christ, all-powerful as it is, is not sufficient. This is not heresy; it is solemn truth, and, reader, the sooner you find it out the better. It may make the matter of sin appear more serious to you. The blood of Christ will wash away the guilt of our sins, if we truly repent and believe, and our hearts may be made as pure as though we had never sinned; but the stain of it lies ever upon our memory, and its somber shadow lies upon our life whenever memory calls it to view. No doubt that shadow will be as eternal as our souls.

Its stain also lies upon our reputation. Men do not forget such things. If you backslide and go into sin, you may obtain salvation again through the forbearance of God, but you can not get away from the stigma of your backsliding. The sins you committed may be forgiven by the saints, for "charity shall cover a multitude of sins," but the world neither forgets nor forgives. The preacher who, after he has preached to others to live right, goes into sin, can not expect repentance to put him back where he was before, except in the mercy of God. He will have his sin to live down. His words will have lost their power. His influence will have greatly suffered.

This is true of others as well as of preachers. David was a man of God; he sinned, and to this day men despise him for it. The skeptic and the infidel cease not to point to the sad spectacle. The one sin of Peter in denying his Lord stands out today as a dark stain upon his life. O my friend, if you have been defeated in your Christian life, if you have lost the sacred treasure of salvation from your heart, I adjure you to-day that you do not throw away everything, but value at their true worth the things that remain to you, and hold them fast. In your righteous life you formed many good habits; do not turn away from them, hold fast to them. You had a thankful and appreciative heart toward God; do not become hard and thankless. You had a reverence for holy things; do not let it go. You had a desire to please God; keep that desire still warm in your bosom. Keep your face turned Godward, not worldward, and make your way back to him at once.

Sometimes people sin against God, then immediately cease their profession and just drift along day after day, making no effort to obtain forgiveness. They think they will "get saved again" when some evangelist comes to hold a revival. We often see reports of meetings saying that so many "backsliders were reclaimed." This expression tells a sad story of such careless living before God that it makes one's heart sad to contemplate it. If Satan gets advantage of you, or your foot slips in your upward climb, do not let go all holds and go clear to the bottom into the pit of sin, there to lie carelessly; do not lose an inch more than you can help losing. If you have sinned, resolutely determine that you will not add to it another sin. Repent of the one committed and press your way right back to God; do not wait for some preacher; do not wait for anything; return to God. To drift along and wait is folly. It is giving Satan all the chance he needs.

One of the most hurtful ideas existing among us today

is, that one sin puts a man back in the same place where
he was before he was saved. Nothing could be more
false; nothing could more obscure what salvation has
done for him. Nothing could tend more to make him
indifferent and careless. I want to oppose that idea
with all my strength, for it is Satan's lie. When a man
sins he becomes guilty, but the good character that has
been built up, the pure feelings and desires, the right
habits of thought and action, the Christian point of view
to which he has attained—these are all a wealth that he
still possesses. They are something of exceeding value,
which in a large measure still remain in his possession.
They are, however, in serious danger. If he persists in
sin, he will lose them all; but if he recovers himself in
time, he will save them.

I offer no excuse for sin; it is terrible, and how quickly
its deadly infection spreads through all the being! Fear
it as you would fear a plague. If you have sinned, make
your way back to God at once before that sin shall "increase to more ungodliness." If you are a backslider,
do not think that it does not matter what you do; for
it does matter greatly. Do not add sin to sin, increasing your guilt; but let the fear of God be upon your
heart. If you are overcome, do not let yourself be
routed. Do not throw away your weapons in a panic,
but turn again and face the foe and fight him until the
victory comes, until you regain what you have lost, until you stand "more than conqueror through him that
loved us."

TALK TWENTY-FIVE

MY DREAM MESSAGE

Solomon says that dreams come "through the multitude of business." Our night thoughts are like our day thoughts, except that our faculties being partly asleep, our dreams usually lack the coherence and the reasonableness of our waking thoughts. God does occasionally, at rare intervals, operate upon men's minds to cause them to dream something; but even the prophets with whom he thus communicated more than with ordinary men received such messages only now and then, and their other dreams had no significance.

Many people are always trying to find some hidden meaning in their dreams. If they have some peculiar dream, they try to interpret it or to get somebody else to do so. Now, God is reasonable. He knows that we can better comprehend when we are awake than when we are asleep; so he usually communicates with us during our waking hours. We sometimes have very striking dreams, but this does not signify that the Lord originated them. I have known people to act very unwisely as the result of following dreams. One night a preacher, who was holding a series of meetings, dreamed of having a terrible fight with a great snake. When he awoke, he felt that surely the Lord was trying to show him something. He interpreted the dream to mean that somebody in the congregation was represented by that snake. The next day he told his dream in the meeting and said that he thought he knew who the snake was. He began acting upon his supposition. The result was that at least two of the congregation backslid over it, and the whole church was thrown into confusion.

A dream is a dream, and possibly not more than one in ten thousand come from God. There are times, however, when we may learn good lessons from our dream thoughts as well as from our waking thoughts. One such dream I once had, and the lesson I derived from it has been good for my soul. I dreamed that I stood beside a gigantic wild rosebush. In my hand I held one of the beautiful fragrant flowers. I looked at it and drank in its rich perfume, but I saw a great number of flowers, and I desired more than the one, so I held it in my left hand and began to reach up for others. They were very high, so I pressed against the outer limbs and stretched to my utmost, but they were too high; I could not get them. I stepped back from the bush. As I did so, my gaze fell upon the rose in my hand just in time to see its petals fall to the ground. In stretching for those beyond my reach, I had ruined the one that was already mine. I gazed upon the empty stem in my hand and at the bruised petals upon the ground with a feeling of regret.

The scene changed. I sat at a desk with pencil and paper, and in my dream wrote these words: "If you have but one rose, enjoy it to the full. Do not let its perfume be wasted upon the empty air, and its beauty go unnoticed, while you spend your time in vain long ing for the unattainable." When I awoke I wrote down the words that I had written in my dream, and through the years they have preached to me many a sermon.

How natural it is for us to forget what we have while we look at others whom we think to be more fortunate! We look at the blessings that others enjoy and forget to be thankful for our own. We look at others' possessions, and because they are greater than ours, we fail to appreciate what we have. Our position in life may be very humble, but however humble, our life is full of blessings if we but have eyes to see them.

When I had this dream, my health was gone, and I lay alone in my bed throughout the long hours of the day while my wife was away working for our support. My eyes were so I could read but a very little. We had two rooms in a house with another family. All around us were people with health and plenty. I could easily realize the difference between my situation and theirs. Sometimes I would look out of the window and see people passing, strong and vigorous and care-free. I would hear the gay laughter and the sound of happy voices, while I—there I lay suffering and alone. How easy it was to see their blessings! and in seeing theirs, how easy it was to forget my own!

But this dream came upon the morning of my birth day; and as I lay there thinking it over, I determined that in the coming year I would not let my one rose be spoiled because I was reaching for that which was beyond my reach. I decided to enjoy my own blessings. If others were more blessed than I, should I not rejoice in the fact? Longing to be like them would not make me so. If I had but little to enjoy, I would enjoy that little. So I began to look at my blessings, and as I looked them over I found them greater than I had supposed. I had

many things to give me comfort. I had food to satisfy
my hunger. I had a home and clothing. I had the
loving care of a faithful wife. I had kind friends who
gave to me freely of their sympathy and who were ready
to grant my every wish so far as it lay in their power.
Better than all else, I had the peace of God in my heart.
I began to realize that my state might be far worse.

The more I thought, the more I saw for which to be
thankful. The more I considered my blessings, the more
I appreciated them. And many a time since have I
looked out upon the passers-by or listened to their mer-
riment, and have said to myself, "I would not exchange
places with you; for I am saved; I have the treasure of
God's love; I have the presence of the Holy Spirit; I
have the joys of salvation; I have a mansion in heaven."
I knew that most of the passers-by did not have these
things, and so I was blessed more than they. What were
health and strength when put to a wrong use? What
were temporal blessings that ministered only to selfishness? What were the joy and gaiety that ignored God?
What were the pleasures of sin, when they only laid
up a harvest of sorrow? Ah no, I had no reason to envy
them, for my blessings were greater and would not fade
away like mist before the sun.

My brother, my sister, you may be happy in your own
little corner if you will learn the lesson of enjoying what
you have. Learn to be content with common things.
Learn that the truest joy does not come from external
things. It springs spontaneously from a contented
heart. If God wills that you be situated as you are, will
he not make you happy where you are? The Bible says,

"Godliness with contentment is great gain . . . Having food and raiment let us be therewith content" (1 Tim. 6:6-8). You may not have much of this world's goods; you may not have many talents; your blessings may seem few; but remember my dream message—"If you have but one rose, enjoy it to the full." If another has both hands filled, he may enjoy them less than you enjoy your one, unless you look with envious eyes. Sometimes a little perfume is sweeter than an abundance. Do not spend your days in vain longing. Do not despise what you have because it is not greater. Cultivate the habit of thankfulness and appreciation. Be glad for what you have. Be contented. Better your condition if you can, but do not spoil what you have in reaching for more. If you have but one talent, use it for the Lord and be thankful for it. Do not depreciate it because others have several talents. Use it and be content. Happiness consists not in the things we have, but in our appreciation and use of them. So enjoy your one rose. Drink in its sweet perfume; gaze upon its beauteous colors. Enjoy it to the full.

TALK TWENTY-SIX

WHEN GOD WITHDRAWS HIMSELF

A mother sat quietly in her easy chair. Upon the floor near her was her little one playing—piling his blocks one upon another, then throwing them down and laughing in childish glee. He was all absorbed in his play. The mother gazed upon him with her eyes beaming. Presently she began to call him, "Baby, come to Mama! Baby, Baby, come to Mama!" but he played on unheeding. Again she called, but he paid no attention; his mind was occupied with his own affairs.

Presently the mother quietly slipped from her chair and went into an adjoining room, out of the baby's sight. He did not notice her go. He supposed that she was right there and that he could go to her at any time; but happening to glance up from his play, he saw that the chair was empty. The laughter ceased at once, and a cloud came over his features; he turned and looked all around the room, but his mama was not in sight. He saw only a stranger sitting in an easy chair. A pang of startled fear passed through him, and he began to cry and call very earnestly, in his baby way, for his mama.

It brought a quick response. The mother, leaving her concealment, rushed to him quickly, picked him up, and hugged him tightly to her bosom. His chubby baby arms were clasped about her neck as though he would never let her go. Soon the tears were gone and the baby's face lay against that of the mother, while the joy of the mother-heart caused the eyes to shine like stars.

Now, the mother did not go away from the child because she did not love it, or because she thought that it did not love her; but she wanted to draw its attention away from its little concerns to herself. She wanted to show her affection for it and to receive its baby caresses in return.

Like that little one, we sometimes become so absorbed in our own pleasures, our work, or some little personal interest, that God can not attract our attention. His father-heart yearns for a season of communion with us. He wants to show his love to us and receive, in turn, our love and communion. But we do not heed him; we are too busy with other things; and so he quietly withdraws himself, and we become aware that we are alone. With that presence gone, how lonely we feel! How dark the world suddenly grows! How quickly we lose interest in the things that held our attention before! How we yearn for his presence again! how our hearts reach out for him! how our tears start! We think, "What have we done that caused him to leave us? have we grieved away his Spirit? have we sinned against him?" But ah! he is not gone far; he is just beyond our vision. He is watching; he is waiting for our hearts to be drawn back to himself.

The mother would not have left her child if by leaving she would have placed him in danger. She did not mean to stay away. So God knows that to leave us thus is not to expose us to danger. He is watching, waiting anxiously the moment when he may return; and ah!

when he does return and takes us in his bosom, what words of comfort he speaks! what tender affection he shows! and how our hearts are melted and poured out in thanksgiving and adoration before him! If God apparently withdraws from us, it is only because he sees that we need to be left alone for a season. He sees that the heart must be drawn away from selfish interest; and when this is accomplished, he comes back and reveals to us anew the fulness and richness of his love.

TALK TWENTY-SEVEN

WHAT HAPPENED TO SOLOMON

In his early manhood Solomon was noted for his deep piety and his fervent love of righteousness. When he became king, he found a great work ready for his hand, and he set about the task with a glad heart. To build a temple to Jehovah was his delight, and he threw into it his whole strength. His prayer at the dedication of the temple shows a deeply reverent and submissive spirit.

As the years went by he increased in riches and honor. His name became a synonym for wisdom. Many nations paid him tribute. But notwithstanding all these things, his heart held true to God. During these years he had, I suppose, no thought but that he should continue thus until the end, that he should live his life out as a true servant of Jehovah, and that his life's sun would go down in a blaze of glory. But alas! it was not so to be. We who know his history know the dark shadow that came over his life. We know how its radiance faded away into the night. We shall do well to analyze the things that led to his downfall.

There was no change in Jehovah. There was no change in Solomon's duty toward him. The change that led to the disaster was in Solomon himself. For political reasons Solomon married princesses of the royal houses round about him. These women were idolaters. Jehovah they regarded as only the national God of the Hebrews. They still clung to their old religions, and wor-

shiped the gods of their nations. Their feelings and
sentiments were all in favor of idolatrous worship. These
influences Solomon withstood for a long time. His heart
held true to God; but these influences kept on working.
He was in daily contact with them, and little by little
they gained a hold upon him; consequently we read,
"It came to pass, when Solomon was old, that his wives
turned away his heart after other gods: and his heart
was not perfect with the Lord his God, as was the heart
of David his father" (1 Kings 11:4). As a result, the
man who had been so honored by God and who had so
honored God became an idolater and put his Lord to an
open shame and drew away into the same net of idola-
try many of his people.

What a lesson there is in this for us! What a warning is there in his example! When young Christians
marry sinners in these days, the final result is generally
pretty much the same as it was with Solomon. But it
is not only through such marriages that hearts are turned
away from the Lord: there are many other things that
will influence us likewise if we are not careful. We are
strongly influenced by the actions of others. That influence is constantly working, whether we are conscious
of it or not. In the life of Joash we see an example of
the power of influence. He was brought up by Jehoiada,
the high priest, who was a man that feared God; and
as a result of the influence brought to bear upon the
young king, he grew up to be a man who feared God,
and who, during the lifetime of Jehoiada, did that which
was right and good in the sight of the Lord. He was
a good king as long as he had a good teacher and was

under proper influence; but at last Jehoiada died, and other influences were brought to bear upon the king. He yielded to them; and instead of continuing to be a godly king, he became a wicked one. Thus, his life experience is parallel to that of Solomon. They were glorious in their youth and young manhood; but in their old days they dishonored their God and themselves, and in consequence their sun went down in darkness, and their lives were blighted and sullied.

With these two examples before us, we shall do well to give heed to the scripture that says, "Let him that thinketh he standeth take heed lest he fall." When we are serving the Lord, it is natural for us to suppose that we shall go right on to the end. We do not think that we shall yield to any influence that will draw us away from the Lord. But alas, how many, like Solomon, are having their hearts turned away by the influences that are brought to bear upon them! Solomon himself said, "Keep thy heart with all diligence," but he failed to do this. The silent and subtile workings of those evil influences wrought in his heart something that he did not know was taking place. He did not realize that he was being alienated from God; but presently his love had waxed cold, his zeal had abated. To him the God of Israel became only as one of the other gods.

There are influences brought to bear upon you each day and each hour, my brother, my sister. Do you know what these influences are? Do you know how they are working? Do you know what effect they are having upon your heart and your life? upon your thoughts and your soul's attitude? Are you diligently guarding yourself against every evil influence? Look into your life and see if there is any evil influence to which you have been gradually and unconsciously yielding. Has the world been getting closer to you through the years? Has it more attraction for you than it had in the days gone by? Do its pride and vanity, its frivolity and ungodliness, seem less obnoxious to you than it has heretofore? Does sin seem a lighter thing to you than it used to? Does the Word of God take less hold upon your conscience now than formerly? Is the voice of duty speaking in your soul in the same clear terms as before? and does it find your soul as ready to respond? Are the service and worship of God still so sweet and satisfying? Is it your delight to give of your substance for the spread of the gospel? or has covetousness, little by little, been working into your heart until it has taken root there? Do you love material things less or more than formerly? Is your consecration just as real and just as complete as it was?

If you are coming short in any of these things, what has been the influence that has worked to bring it about? Make a good, careful examination of the situation. If you have been drifting, beware lest your heart be entirely turned away from the Lord. Find out what influences are working. Watch and defend your heart against them; overcome their influences; counteract their powers; stand for God. It is only in this way that you can serve him to the end faithfully, and that you can be triumphant when the call comes for you to stand before his presence.

TALK TWENTY-EIGHT

FIGHTING THE GOOD FIGHT OF FAITH

Paul said, "Fight the good fight of faith." This world is a battle-ground of spiritual forces. If we are spiritual beings, it is impossible that we should hold ourselves neutral and stand apart from those forces that are in conflict. We must stand on one side or the other of the battle array. Jesus has said, "He that is not with me is against me." Since we must be in the conflict whether we will to be or not, it behooves us to be on the right side. When we know that we are on the right side, then the thing of greatest importance to us is the method of our warfare. Since we wrestle not against flesh and blood, but against the principalities and powers of evil, it is not strange that our weapons should be "not carnal" weapons, which are effective against material foes, but those spiritual weapons that are "mighty through God."

One great outstanding fact in this battle of life is that it is necessarily a battle of faith. As I observe some people's methods of trying to fight this Christian warfare, it seems to me that they are rather fighting the fight of unbelief, or of doubts. Instead of being confident with the confidence that true faith gives, they are all the time fearful. They are never certain they are going to win. They are never certain that their methods are going to prevail. They are always trembling and uncertain. When they do gain a victory, it seems more like a piece of good fortune than the result of their fighting. When they see a conflict coming, they shrink from it and look for some way to evade it. They are filled with fear of the outcome. Sometimes they fight in desperation and win; and when they see that they have won, they are surprized. They were almost sure that they would lose the battle; they were almost certain of defeat, but in some way they won. That victory, however, does not give them much courage to meet the next conflict. They meet it with the same fearfulness, with the same unbelief, with the same doubt. There is not the joyful note of victory in their song. They do not face the future with confident expectation of winning. They are continually harassed with their doubts; they are constantly troubled with forebodings. It is better to fight thus than not to fight at all, but there is a better way than this to fight.

Faith is the mightiest of all weapons. When our spirits are armed with faith, we may go confidently into any battle. We may have expectation of winning. We may know before we fight that victory is ours. We may face our adversary with calm confidence and with a consciousness of an indwelling power that is greater than his power. Has not God said, "Greater is he that is in you, than he that is in the world"? If our faith claims that to be so, then God will make it so to us.

We must have faith in God. He is our leader. The army that does not have confidence in the ability and courage of its leader is half defeated before it goes into battle. Most of us, I think, have confidence in God's ability as a leader, and in his power and wisdom, and believe that he is able to overcome our foes. It is not his ability that we doubt. The only question that confronts us is, "Will he use that power to conquer our enemies?" We see that he has made many promises. It is easy to believe, in a general way, that they will be fulfilled; but when it comes to making direct applications to the situations that we meet, it is there that faith sometimes fails. Will God fight for us on this special occasion? Will God help us now? Will he really make good his word to us? or will he fail us in the critical moment?

If God's promises are true, then the ones that relate to our particular needs are true, and they are true now. If they are true to others, they are true to us, for God is no respecter of persons. And if they are true to us, they are true to us now as well as they were yesterday or will be tomorrow. It is so easy to think that God would help others. They are more worthy than we are. Do you feel this way? Do you feel that if it were somebody else in your place, you could easily have faith that God would help? Then, why not have faith that God will help you?

This brings us to the next important thought: We must have faith in ourselves as well as in God. We must have faith in our integrity and loyalty. Do we mean real business for God? Have we thrown ourselves unreservedly on the side of God in this battle? Do we intend with all our souls to fight the good fight of faith? Do we have it really settled that we are going to do the right? So many *want* to do the right, but they are not sure that they *will* do it. They mean to do it, but they are constantly afraid that they will fail in doing it. This is not faith. Have confidence in yourself; not only in your loyalty and integrity and purpose to serve God, but also in your ability to do it. You can do it. You can do it as well as any one else. That doubt and fearfulness that you have will only be a hindrance to you. Get rid of it. Develop confidence in yourself—not overconfidence that depends upon yourself, but that true confidence that depends upon God helping you and that arms you with courage and trust in God and in yourself.

You must also have confidence in your weapons. Our weapons are "mighty through God," we are told. God has told you how to win; and just as surely as you follow his instructions and trust in him for results, he will cause you to wear the victor's crown. Our cause is a righteous one. Have faith in that cause, and know that right must triumph. But remember that you can not win unless you put your faith into your fighting. "This is the victory that overcometh the world, even your faith." Believe that you will win. No matter how weak you are, no matter how great your foe, no matter what may confront you, go into the conflict with that courage that is born of faith. Believe that God will give you the victory. Do not consider defeat at all. Let your faith mount up, and say: "I can win, and I will win. In God I will conquer." Throw away your doubts. Make an end of them. Trust in God. His Word is true. You can believe it if you will, and believing it, you shall be more than conqueror through him that loves you.

TALK TWENTY-NINE

HOW ARE YOUR EAR CONNECTIONS?

A telephone must be properly connected with where the person is to whom we wish to communicate, or it will be of no value to us. If the connection is broken, or the receiver out of order, it will be useless for us to talk into the transmitter: the person at the other end will hear none of our words. We may speak just the same as though he were hearing, but nothing will be accomplished. There must be a proper connection: there must be a responsive vibration at the other end of the wire.

It is just so in spiritual things. One of the most important things is to have our ears properly connected with our hearts. We have often heard the expression, "It just went in at one ear and out at the other." By this is meant that the one who heard gave no heed. How often this occurs in regard to the things of God!

When it comes to gossip and idle tales and foolish conversation and things of that sort, we ought to let such go "in at one ear and out at the other"; we should be very careful that they find no lodging-place in our hearts. That is the only safe way for our souls. But too often these things are given a place in the heart and mind: there is too good a connection, and many times there is only too ready a response in the heart for such things. That is why some people can never keep spiritual, and are always lagging behind others. People who have such a good connection and responsiveness in their hearts on these lines usually have very poor connection between their ears and their hearts when it comes to the teachings of the Word of God. They can hear the Word preached on almost any subject, and not seem to think it means them. They go along in their lives just as they had been doing before. They feel no particular responsibility to obey. They can go on just as if they had never heard, and still profess, and possibly shout occasionally.

There were times when Israel had their connection broken. God said to the prophet of old, "They hear thy words, but they will not do them." So many times people say, "Was not that a good sermon today?" Why, yes, how they enjoyed it! But they go their way and give no further heed to what was said. However, in the popular pulpits of today the preachers too often hold this attitude: "This is my opinion of things. You may take it or let it alone, just as you please; you have a right to your own opinions about it." And there are a great many people who act upon this idea. They feel that they can take a thing or let it alone, just as they please—even when the words preached are the judgments of God. Many hold that attitude not only toward preaching but toward the Bible also. They read, or hear read, what it says about worldliness, foolish actions and conversation, the wearing of gold for adornment; they read about being patient and holy and blameless, about not returning evil for evil, and about speaking evil of no man; yet they go right on doing the things forbidden, just as though the Book said nothing. They do not take it to heart. The trouble is, the connections between their ears and their hearts are broken as far as these things of God are concerned.

The Bible warns us to take heed how we hear. If we do not treat the preaching of God's Word reverently, and listen with reverent hearts to his messages, it is because we do not reverence him. It is because in our hearts we are lifted up against him. That attitude of "I shall take or leave alone, just as I please" is one of the very worst attitudes that can be held. Not only is it dishonoring to God, but it is exceedingly dangerous.

Sometimes such an attitude of heart is partly, at least, the result of the way the preacher preaches. If a man has a message from God, he has authority to preach that message as the word of God, and he should so preach it. Every true gospel preacher should be imbued with the feeling: "I am preaching the truth of God. It is your duty to hear it; I expect you to hear it; and hear it you must." Let him hold this attitude in his heart and mind, and then let him enforce upon his congregation by proper disciplinary methods the truth that he preaches. If the preacher feels his authority as God's spokesman as he ought to feel it, the people will be impressed—they can not help it. It is true that they may rebel, grow stubborn, or disobey; they may shut his words out from their hearts; but nevertheless he is clear, and they only increase their responsibility, of which they must give an account to God. Paul believed that preaching and teaching should be with "all authority." This does not imply mere human rule, but divine authority—God speaking through the man.

When the heart does not hear and feel, there is always a reason. One reason is self-will. People do not like to be told what to do. They like to be masters of themselves. God's government demands complete surrender of self-will and must of necessity do so. If we will be his servants, it is not for us to choose what our lives shall be, nor what we shall say, nor what we shall do. It is his right to command; it is our part to hear and to obey. To hear and then to heed just as we please is setting up our authority above his. The two ideas of service and self-will are opposed the one to the other. Self-will always means rebellion against God's will. Therefore if a person chooses what he will do, and leaves undone what he finds distasteful, he, and not God, is the master. This self-willed disposition is very noticeable among nominal professors of religion. They profess to be God's servants, and yet they set their wills not to do certain things that they ought to do, or else to do certain things that they ought not to do. They have their minds and hearts set in the matter. When they hear the Word of God preached on matters predetermined by them, it falls on unhearing ears. There is no response of the heart.

Another reason is love of ease—indolence. People hear the voice of duty, but they do not respond to it because they do not wish to make the necessary effort. They do not let their hearts be pressed by a sense of duty on that particular point, because to obey they must arouse themselves from their indolent attitude.

One symptom showing that the heart does not hear is unbelief. One reason why the Jews did not believe Christ was because their hearts were so hard, and that is one reason why people do not hear the gospel in these days. This is not confined to non-professing sinners;

it is a very common thing among church-members. Reader, how is it with you? Are you one of those who have the connection broken between the ears and the heart? or have you listening ears and a feeling heart? When you hear the Word of God preached on certain subjects, can you slight it? or does it sink deep into your conscience and take hold there and produce fruit in your life? Are you ready to live by every word of God? or do you want to take only that which suits your views? If the latter is true in your case, you are in a dangerous condition. God has the word preached, not simply to entertain people, but that they may obey it. The soul who delights in God's will does not have to be compelled to listen, nor does he have to be compelled to obey; he is ready both to hear and to obey. If there is something wrong with the connection between your ears and your heart, you had better get one of God's "trouble men" to look after it at once; or, better still, go direct to God and have the connection remade. Get your heart taught to feel as it ought to feel, and to respond as it ought to respond. Be not a hearer only, but be a doer of God's Word.

TALK THIRTY

FRET NOT THYSELF

To fret means to chafe, to be irritated, to be uneasy, to be troubled and bothered. It is just the opposite of peaceful, trustful rest. Jesus has promised us rest to our souls, and we may have this rest. We can not have it, however, if we give place to worrying and fretting. God's purpose for us is that we shall have calmness and soul-quietness, even in the midst of tribulation. He has said, "My peace I give unto you." He followed this by saying, "Let not your heart be troubled, neither let it be fearful" (John 14:27). (These and all following quotations are from the American Standard Version.)

It is not God's will that we be continually worrying. This world is full of things that are not as they ought to be, and if we are to be happy and peaceful we must adjust ourselves to circumstances and learn to be happy in spite of the things that are displeasing to us, that are not as they ought to be. We can never be amidst ideal conditions in this world.

Fretting is like sand in a bearing; it is likely to make all sorts of trouble. It will use up the energy that we ought to be using for something else; it will keep our physical and spiritual nerves on edge; it will spoil the tranquility of our lives; it will mar our peace and take the sweetness out of our devotions.

Some people are always worrying about the wrong-doings of others. They fret and grieve, and can not remove the subject from their minds nor the burden

from their hearts. The Bible says, ''Fret not thyself
because of evil-doers'' (Psa. 37:1). Many people choose
to do wrong; many people do wrong to themselves and
to others, including God's people. Of course, we can not
rejoice over this, but we should not let it spoil our own
lives. We should not fret about it. We should have
a proper concern for the welfare of their souls, so that
we shall earnestly pray for them and do all in our
power to cause them to do better, but this is very different from being fretful, from worrying and bothering
ourselves continually. If we keep our eyes on the wickedness of others and continually grieve over it, we shall
have no time to be joyful ourselves, we shall have no
time to live our life with God.

Psalm 37 further says, ''Fret not thyself because of
him who prospereth in his way, because of the man
who bringeth wicked devices to pass'' (v. 7). What
all of us need to learn is to let God bear his own re-
sponsibilities. He tells us what to do in the first part
of the verse—''Rest in Jehovah, and wait patiently for
him.'' If evil-doers prosper, if they seem even more
prosperous than the righteous, if they seem to get along
without trouble, we should not be bothered over that.
That is God's business. We see a great many evil
things going on, and we should like to stop them. They
grieve us in spirit, and this is but natural. But we
ought not to fret ourselves over them. There is a vast
difference between godly concern and human worry, and
we need to learn this difference clearly. To be concerned about such things, and to pray earnestly for
God to overcome them and put a stop to them, is all

very well; but when it comes to fretting over them and worrying and being bothered, this is quite another thing. We should never let these things mar the peace of our souls. God means for us to have peace and be thankful right here in the midst of all this wickedness.

He tells us why we should not fret. "Fret not thyself; it tendeth only to evil-doing" (v. 8). Fretfulness has a tendency to make us doubt God and his wisdom: how natural for us to think that if we had the power that he has we would put a stop to such things. It has a tendency to make us murmur and to be dissatisfied. It is likely to discourage us; and when we are discouraged, we are likely to murmur against the way things appear to be going. Fretfulness is almost certain to take the sweetness out of our hearts and out of our communion with God. It will lead to a loss of spirituality. It will rob us of spiritual tone.

When we are fretting we may think that we are doing the best we can, but we are not. We may think that we can not help fretting, but we can. There is a way in which we may possess control of ourselves and cast the burden of the responsibility upon God, and he will bear it if we do thus. We have to decide that we will be happy no matter what happens, no matter what the conduct of others may be, no matter what obstacles they place in our way, no matter what burdens they may throw upon us. We will be happy anyway, because God has willed that we should be happy. If we see things going wrong we should take the burden to the Lord, saying: "Lord, thou must bear the responsibility of these things. My shoulders were not made to bear these

burdens. They are thine. I give them over to thee.
If anything is to be accomplished, thou must do it."
Then we must take our hands off. We must let the thing
go, treat it as something that is none of our business,
and let God handle the situation.

Again, he said, "Neither be thou envious against them
that work unrighteousness." It is so easy to look upon
those who are rich and who are not using their money
for God, and think, "I wish I had their money; how
much good I might do with it!" Or perhaps when we
see talented people of the world, we might say, "Oh, if
I had the ability they have, I would use it for the Lord!"
God does not want us to do this; that is, to envy them
their riches or their talents. It is all right for us to wish
that we had more money or greater talents to use for
the Lord, but it is not right to be envious of others.
Even wishing that we had more is a waste of time.
The thing that is important is that we use what we do
have.

If we are given to letting ourselves worry and fret
over things that others do toward us, it is often an in-
centive to them to try to make us trouble. We see a
good illustration of this in the life of Hannah. Elkanah
had two wives. Peninnah had a number of children,
but Hannah was childless. Peninnah took advantage of
this to reproach Hannah, and it is said she "provoked
her sore, to make her fret" (1 Sam. 1: 6). There are
some people who delight in twitting others about some
fault or physical defect, or because of lack of ability or
something of that sort. If they see that this causes us
to fret, it only increases their desire to provoke us. Then

again, some people like to make sport of others, and tease them; and if they see that some one can not bear it well, if it frets him and worries him, this only increases their delight. I have heard such people say, "I just like to tease So-and-so; he can not stand it at all." Saints, of course, should never do such a thing as that; they should have more regard for the feelings of others. But sinners will do such things. We may expect it. Therefore, the thing to do is to learn not to fret over it, but to submit our ways to God and bear it patiently.

Never allow yourself to fret over anything. Fretting never helps. It always hinders. Learn to commit these things to God. Cast your burdens upon him—and do not try to bear his burdens. Learn to be happy in spite of your difficulties. Keep your own soul-life separated from these troublesome things. God will help you, and you can make a success. He commands you not to fret, and he will give you grace to keep from doing it.

TALK THIRTY-ONE

BEING EASILY ENTREATED

Not long since I saw in the report of a meeting a statement something like this: "The brethren were easily entreated, and so all personal difficulties were easily settled." One of the greatest problems that ministers meet· and one that requires the most patience and wisdom is the problem of settling personal difficulties. These difficulties are often found existing between those professing to be Christians. And sometimes they are very hard to get settled. There is just one reason for this: those involved are not "easy to be entreated." James tells us that this is a quality of that "wisdom that is from above." The quality of being easily entreated is a mark of true piety and of a Christlike spirit. Where it is wanting, spirituality is always below normal. It is not hard to settle troubles if people want to have them settled; for if they really want them settled, they are willing to settle them the right way. Peace and harmony mean more to them than any other consideration, except truth. Division and discord can not exist unless people are willing to have it so; that is, unless one or both parties place a higher value upon something else than they do upon peace and harmony.

Abraham is an example of a man who is easily en-treated. When strife arose between his herdmen and those of Lot, it grieved him, and he said to Lot, "Let there be no strife, I pray thee, between me and thee, and between my herdmen and thy herdmen; for we be

brethren" (Gen. 13:8). He therefore proposed to give
Lot his choice of all the land and to take what was left.

What does it mean to be easily entreated? It means
to be kind and just and reasonable and self-sacrificing in
one's attitude toward others. The man who possesses
this quality habitually manifests this temper in his life.
There are those who are very tenacious of their rights.
They feel that people do not respect those rights as they
should; so when any question involving them arises, they
feel as though they must "stand up for their rights."
They often lose sight of everything else; kindness, mercy,
forbearance, patience, Christlikeness—in fact, nothing
counts but their rights. Their rights they will defend;
and very often their rights prove to be wrongs, or in
insisting on their rights they do that which wrongs
others. Really spiritual people are not so particular
and insistent concerning their rights. They would far
rather sacrifice their rights than to contend for them,
unless something vital is involved, which is rarely the
case. When a spiritual man is compelled to defend his
rights, he will do it in a meek and quiet way, a way that
has in it nothing offensive or self-assertive. When they
were about to scourge Paul unlawfully, his only assertion of his rights was to quietly ask, "Is it lawful for
you to scourge a man that is a Roman, and uncon-
demned?" (Acts 22:25). But there are those who will
not yield in the least; they know their rights, and they
will not yield to any one! Very often their rights would
look quite different if such persons possessed more of
the spirit of Christ.

Things sometimes look very different to different people, and no amount of talking and arguing will make them see alike; and the more of such there is, the further apart people drift. That is the reason so many church troubles are always *being* settled but are never *really* settled. The trouble is in the hearts. The members are not willing to be entreated. Let them get their hearts warm toward each other, and be filled with the spirit of brotherly kindness. Until such is the condition, one might as well try to weld two pieces of cold iron. As before stated, when people desire unity and harmony they can have it. But they must desire it enough to be willing to sacrifice for it all those things that prevent it.

Another thing that hinders is self-will. So many people like to have their own way. If others will do their way, such persons can be very gracious and kind; but if they do not have their way, they manifest a very different disposition. They are ready to "balk"; their kindness is gone; they become stubborn; if there is trouble, they are very slow to yield. It is very hard for them to submit even when they are convinced that they should do so. When they do seem to yield, it is often only an outward yielding, the heart remaining the same. How much trouble this self-will makes, and how different it is in spirit from him who said, "Not my will, but thine, be done"! We are commanded to submit ourselves one to another. When we demand that all the submission be on the part of the other person, it shows that we are self-willed, that we care more about having things go our way than we do about having them go right, or than we care to manifest a Christlike disposition.

Still another thing that prevents our being easily

entreated is pride. A lady was recently talking with me about a conversation she had just had with some other ladies. She had been advocating a certain doctrine which they did not receive. In speaking of it she said: "I grew a little warm in the discussion of it. I did not mean to let them best me." So many people have this disposition. They will not be "bested." They will hold to their position even when they are in the wrong, and know it. If they did not take such a position, they might acknowledge the other to be right; but when they have taken the stand, they will not yield. What is the trouble? Pride in the heart is the secret. This disposition always has its root in pride; humility never acts in this way. Pride keeps people from acknowledging truth; it keeps them from changing their attitude. Pride of opinion keeps them from being willing to listen patiently to others who differ with them. Pride is at the root of many church and personal troubles; pride is what they feed on, and the only way to cure them is to get rid of the pride.

The minister who would settle such troubles has need to look for one or more of these three things. He may expect a search to disclose either selfishness, self-will, or pride; for if the trouble is not easily settled, he may be assured that some or all of them are in the way. His task, then, is not so much to get at what seems to be the trouble, as to give attention to these underlying things which are the life of the trouble. No trouble is truly settled till these elements are purged out of the heart.

O brethren! what we need in all the churches and in every heart is that "wisdom that is from above" (Jas.

3:17). We are told that it is "first pure." By wisdom James does not here mean what we usually mean by that term, but in it he includes the whole of the gift of God that comes to us in our salvation. It is "first pure," then as a natural consequence of that purity it is "peaceable." It loves peace; it seeks to be at peace with all. It is "gentle." That gentleness which was manifested in the life of Jesus reveals itself anew in the hearts of those who are "first pure." Love has no harsh words, no harsh feelings. It is full of mercy and easy to be entreated. Where this heavenly wisdom abides, there will not be a disposition to assert one's own rights, to be self-willed, or to hold fast to one's own ways; on the contrary, if its blessed presence fills our souls, we shall be merciful, kind, forgiving, long-suffering, pitiful, and we shall have the same tender feeling for our brother who has done us wrong as the father had for the prodigal. We shall be ready to run to meet him. We shall be ready to forget all the past. Our hearts will be filled with joyfulness at the expected reconciliation. O brethren there is nothing needed quite so much today and every day as that heart-quality that makes people "easy to be entreated."

TALK THIRTY-TWO

FOLLOWING "WHITHERSOEVER"

One day as Jesus was passing along the highway, a man said to him, "I will follow thee whithersoever thou goest" (Luke 9: 57). This man no doubt was greatly impressed by the wonderful works and noble character of Christ. He thought that companionship with such a man would be full of blessing and richness. Just to see and hear would be worth any man's time and effort—to hear the gracious words that came from His lips would enrich mind and heart; to see the mighty works done would inspire. To him it seemed to be one of the most desirable of all things. Christ's answer to him, however, showed that following Him might well mean something more than this man had ever considered. His way did not always lead through pleasant places; His path was not always to be rose-strewn; not always would the multitude look on Him with favor. Whether this man followed Jesus we are not told, but following evidently meant more to him now than it had meant before.

There are many today who, like that man of old, say, "Lord, I will follow thee," with no clear idea of what it means. It was not hard to follow him when the multitude shouted, "Hosanna!" and threw palm-branches before him. It is easy for us to follow him today when his cause is popular, when people are proclaiming the truth of what we teach and approving of our service. It is no task to follow when it brings praise and admiration. It is no task to follow in the calm after his "Peace, be still," on Gennesaret. Who would not follow gladly to the mount of transfiguration to behold his glory? But to follow him "whithersoever" means more than this.

It is our privilege to share in his glory, his triumph, and his exaltation; but if we have a part in these, as true followers we must also follow him in his humiliation. Are we willing to follow him when the multitude laughs and mocks at him? when his cause is unpopular? when for praise we have reproaches? when for smiles we have sneers?* Then comes the test whether we will follow him all the way.

On one occasion, after he had preached, the multitude forsook him and only the Twelve were stedfast. In these days many are offended at the Word. Are we willing to accept it all? Are we willing to listen to it all? Are we willing to obey it all? God wants "whithersoever" men and women, who will hear the whole Word, believe the whole Word, and obey the whole Word. If we shrink from obedience to any part, we lack just that much of being "whithersoever" disciples. Christ lived a dedicated life; he was dedicated to his Father's will and accomplished his work; he gave himself solely to this. He allowed nothing to come between him and the fulfilment of God's purpose. With him nothing counted except that he should finish his work.

There is a purpose, a moving purpose, in every life. There is one thing above all other things that is the chief purpose of our life. In many cases that purpose is to please self, to follow out a course of our own choosing. The dominant purpose in the heart of every true follower is the same as it was in the life of Christ—to do the will and work of the Father. He who shrinks from either may hesitate to call himself a true follower. Christ sacrificed all, even his life. A ''whithersoever'' follower has the same spirit of sacrifice; he will not withhold himself nor that which is his. The early church rejoiced ''that they were counted worthy to suffer'' for Christ. Let us today look into our own hearts and see if we are animated by the same spirit. That spirit is a very different spirit from that which is seen in those who are offended by a word or a look and who are ready to resent the slightest act that encroaches upon their rights. How empty the claim of many who profess to be real followers! They follow where it pleases them, but as soon as something happens not to their liking, they are ready to draw back.

Christ had not where to lay his head. We have no record that he ever owned anything save the clothes he wore. A ''whithersoever'' follower is not ashamed of the poor; and if he himself is poor, he is not ashamed of his poverty. But Christ was not always poor. We read that ''he became poor.'' He sacrificed that others might be enriched. The same spirit of sacrifice will make us willing to sacrifice what we have for the enrichment of others. If there were more ''whithersoevers'' among us, we should not hear of ministers' being kept out of the work through lack of support or a lack of funds to carry on the Lord's work. Think of a stingy ''whithersoever''! Can you imagine such a combination? Yet many professed followers fail in their duty to give to the cause.

Let us bring the question home to ourselves. Let us

examine our hearts and lives. Are we willing to follow Christ all the way, even when we are rejected by our friends and relatives, through sneers and revilings? We might be willing to walk on the waters with him, but how about Gethsemane? We may be willing to eat of the loaves and fishes, but are we willing to go with him to the palace of the high priest? We might drink of the wine of Cana, but will we wear the thorns? We would gladly sit with him on his throne, but will we bear the cross with him to Calvary? We can easily follow him where the way is easy and when our emotions are exalted and our hearts full of praise, but will we follow him when the skies grow dark, when we are troubled, when bitter trials come, when it takes courage to face what is before us? Let us decide to be true when the way is strewn with stones or hedged with thorns, when the clouds hang low as well as when all is bright and encouraging. Let us cast away all shrinking, and say from our hearts and by our lives, "I will follow whithersoever thou goest."

TALK THIRTY-THREE

PAUL'S PERSUASION

Paul uses the term "persuaded" in the sense of
assurance. When he said that he was persuaded of a
thing involving God's attitude, he meant that he was
fully convinced that it was as it was stated to be. He
meant that to him it stood out as a reality. It was a
thing that he no longer questioned. In Rom. 8:38 and
39, he speaks of one of the things of which he was
persuaded. He did not seem to feel about it as some
feel; and when they read what he says, they realize that
they do not feel just as he did. He says, "For I am
persuaded, that neither death, nor life, nor angels, nor
principalities, nor powers, nor things present, nor
things to come, nor height, nor depth, nor any other
creature, shall be able to separate us from the love of
God, which is in Christ Jesus our Lord."

Some people are all the time worrying lest they should
be separated from that love, lest God's love should be
turned into hatred against them. They walk before him
with fear and trembling. They are all the time questioning whether their conduct merits his approval. They
are ever fearful lest they might do something that would
bring his wrath upon them. Their life is a life of fear
and of bondage. Paul had no such fears and no such
feelings. He knew that the great heart of God is a
heart of love, a heart of tender pity, compassion, and
sympathy. He knew that God is tender toward his

earthly children. Why, even when we were sinners, Christ died for us! and the Father so loved us that he gave his only begotten Son. This love was for rebels. How much greater his affection for his sons! Instead of thinking that he might be easily separated from the love of God, and that he should have to be exceedingly careful lest he should be, Paul cries out, "Who shall separate us from the love of Christ?" (v. 35). By this he means, Who or what *shall be able* to separate us?

Paul knew something of the strength of earthly love. He knew mother-love—how tenderly it holds to its own. He knew that no matter where the son wanders, mother-love goes with him; mother-love calls him back; mother-love yearns over him. He knew love in other forms— how tenaciously it clings to its objects. But the love of Christ, or the love of God in Christ, is above and beyond all this human love. And so he cried out, "Who shall separate us from the love of Christ?" Then he named some things and asked if they should separate us from God's love, and when he looked at them all, he was still persuaded that nothing should be able.

Paul says, "Neither death nor life." If death should lay his icy fingers upon us, it would be but the ushering into the more immediate presence of that great love. But if we must continue to live on in our earthly circumstances and surroundings, that very life can not separate us from the love of Christ, for he will love us through it all. Through various changes, through all the trying situations that may face us, that love will hold us fast. Time and change can not make that love grow cold.

Again, he says, "Nor angels." God is in heaven, surrounded by the angels, but he wants us to understand that those angels can not take up so much of his time and attention that he will forget us. Nor can those evil angels that hate God and hate us separate between us and his love. Even Satan himself, their leader and master, has not power to come between us and the love of God. Ah, soul, do not be afraid. Satan has no knife sharp enough to cut that love. He has no strength to tear its tendrils out of our hearts. He can not burn those cords that hold us. Even all his legions can not touch that love, if we trust it and trust ourselves in God's keeping.

Then he says, "Nor things present." O my brother, sister, do you believe that? Do you believe that the things of this hour, whatever they may be, can not separate you from the love of God? "Things present." How many things there are present. How many things there are that press in upon us! How many discouragements there are in life! How many perplexities! How many things that trouble! How many things that would draw us away! Yet, if we keep our trust in God, none of these things will be able to separate us from his love. None of these things will make him turn his back upon us.

"Nor things to come." Do you look into the future with dread? Do you see with forebodings the things that appear there? Do you think, "How shall I ever pass through it? How shall I ever overcome?" Ah, those things that are ahead of you can not separate you from God's love. That love is going to securely hold

you through them all. That love is going to be your
strength and your safeguard, your hope and your all.
Cast away your forebodings. Look to God with confidence until the confidence of Paul enters your soul and
you can say with the same assurance that he did, "I am
persuaded."

Again, he says, "Nor height, nor depth." It matters
not if God is in heaven, high above us. It matters not
if he is so great, so majestic, so powerful. His height
above us shall not prevent his love from reaching us
and holding us up. "Nor depth." It matters not to
what depth we sink, whether it be depths of discouragement or depths of fear or depths in the feeling of
our own helplessness. It matters not if God is very
high and we are very low, if he is very great and we
are very small; our depth shall not separate us from
his height. His love will bridge the gulf.

O soul, trust in that love. Rely upon it. It will
never fail you. It will securely hold you in the gales
of life. Tribulation or distress or persecution or famine
or nakedness or perils or storms—none of these things
shall be able to separate you from him. And the apostle
continues to say, "Nay, in all these things we are more
than conquerors through him that loved us" (v. 37).
Love will bear us up as with eagles' wings. It will make
smooth the rough paths. It will give strength to the
fainting heart. It will preserve us while in the midst
of temptation; and even when we have come short of
our expectations, when we realize that we have in a
measure failed, that love will not cast us off, but will
hold us safe and secure until the end. Let us look to

that love, and be confident, and rest in full assurance
of faith, knowing that

> When the storm-winds rage, and the rain falls fast,
>   And the clouds hang low above,
> I shall be secure till the storm is past,
>   For I trust my Savior's love,
> And he knows the way, and he holds my hand,
>   And he will not let it go;
> He will lead me home to that better land
>   Just because he loves me so.
>
> I will trust his love, for it e'er will last;
>   It is rich and warm and free;
> Through the years of life it will hold me fast,
>   And my help and comfort be.
> To my waiting heart all its treasures rare,
>   As a sparkling stream shall flow;
> In the joy of God I shall ever share,
>   Just because he loves me so.

TALK THIRTY-FOUR

IN CHRIST AND IN EPHESUS

Paul addressed his Ephesian epistle, "To the saints which are *at Ephesus*, and to the faithful *in Christ Jesus.*" The people addressed were in Ephesus, and they were likewise in Christ. What did it mean to be in Ephesus? Ephesus was one of the great centers of paganism. It was adorned with costly and magnificent temples. It was rich and voluptuous. Both private and public life were utterly corrupt. Even the religious practises of the Ephesians were unspeakably vile. This city was a moral bog, a sink of pollution, filled with all corruption, and reeking with vileness. It was a second Sodom. Vice stalked abroad everywhere and was honored and worshiped.

We might therefore well say, "Can any good thing come out of Ephesus? Can Christianity flourish in such surroundings?" But there were saints in Ephesus, and faithful ones, too. They were such in their lives and characters as to win the commendation of that great apostle to the Gentiles. Out of that obnoxious mud of iniquity were growing the pure white lilies of Christian character. That is the glory of Christianity and of Christ. Those who were now Christians were not superior to the other Ephesians; they were not by nature different. In fact, Paul tells them that they had been the children of wrath, even as others, and that they had been such by nature. What a triumph of divine grace that raised these people up out of such unspeakable filth and made them faithful saints! And yet that is the power of our great Christ.

Some persons look around at the present condition of things in this world, at sin abounding on every hand, and say, "There is no use for me to try to be a Christian or to be different from the others." There are many who look at things in this way. They think it useless to try to be righteous under present conditions. Once while walking down the street of a certain city, I came upon a policeman standing on the street-corner. I engaged him in conversation, which I quickly turned into religious channels, and began inquiring about his own standing. He said to me in a hopeless voice, "Oh, there is no use talking; there is no chance for a policeman." I tried to tell him of the power of God and of what salvation would do for him. But it seemed as an idle tale to him, and he could only reply, "There is no hope for a policeman."

There are many other people today in various situations who say: "There is no hope for me. There is no use for me to try." Those Ephesians might have talked the same way. They had just as much reason to do so as any one else. Probably some of them did talk like that and were lost; who can tell? There were a great many, however, who turned from idols to serve the true and living God, received Christ into their hearts, and found the power of salvation in the gospel. They found power in the blood of Christ to cleanse them from their impurities, and not only so, but also to raise them so far from the mire of sin and wickedness abounding around them as to keep them faithful in Christ Jesus while still dwelling in Ephesus.

It is not so much a change of environment that people need as a change of heart and of character. Diamonds are often found embedded in volcanic mud; mud surrounds them on every side, and yet they have lain there for centuries and are still diamonds. What is the secret of it? Why have they not become contaminated? It is because the mud never entered the diamond; and that was the reason that the Ephesian saints could be faithful and still live in Ephesus. They were left amidst the foul mud of corruption, but the mud was taken out of them, and the grace of Christ kept it from getting back in again.

We can not get away from the mud and defilement of sin in this world. Sin will ever be all about us. Its stench will be in our nostrils from day to day. Our eyes will be offended by it, and our ears will be shocked. But so long as we keep it all on the outside, we can be saints and faithful in Christ Jesus. We are told that one of the chief things for us to do is to keep ourselves "unspotted from the world." Phil. 2:15 says, "That ye may be blameless and harmless, the sons of God, without rebuke, in the midst of a crooked and perverse nation, among whom ye shine as lights in the world." Again Paul says, "Neither be partakers of other men's sins: keep thyself pure" (1 Tim. 5:22). We are not only to keep free from committing any sins of our own, but also to avoid partaking of the sins of others. That is very important.

Now, we are, as it were, in Ephesus. There is sin

abounding all about us. God wants us so to abhor the sins of others that we shall not follow them, nor find pleasure in those who do sinful things. There are two ways in which we can partake of other people's sins. One way is to approve of their evil works. It may be that we ourselves would not do those things, but if we approve of some one else's doing them, it is just about as bad.

Never allow yourself to approve of another's sins. You can not keep clean and do it. Again, we may be partakers of other men's sins by partaking of the results of them. If a man cheats another in business, and then I share in his ill-gotten gain, I am partaking of his sin. It may be that I would not steal my neighbor's melons; but if another steals them, and I, knowing his theft, eat of them with him, do I not partake of his sins? And so it is with all the affairs of life.

We must keep ourselves separate from sin. We can not help being in Ephesus. We must live in this corrupt and sinful world. So the important thing is that we attend to keeping ourselves in Christ—unspotted from the world. If the Ephesians could do this, so can we. But to do it, we must walk uprightly. We must not stoop down into the mire of sin, but keep ourselves erect, and keep our spiritual nostrils above the poisonous gases of sin.

Lot was a man of God. He dwelt in Sodom, and we are told that his righteous soul was vexed from day to day because of the wicked conduct of the Sodomites. But he kept himself clear; he had no part with them; he hated their sins. When we reach a place where we do not hate sin, where we can see it and hear and know of it and find no vexation in our souls, it causes us no uneasiness, we have no particular repugnance for it, it is time that we were becoming awakened. We are commanded to abhor that which is evil, and it is only by so doing and by keeping ourselves clean from it that we can be safe in Christ Jesus and dwell in this wicked world.

There was a bit of heaven in every Christian heart in Ephesus. That bit of heaven was just as pure as the celestial realms above. We too have that heavenly element in our hearts; and in that transplanted bit of God's holiness will flourish all the plants of righteousness that bloom in the courts eternal. But we must guard these plants by keeping the gates of our hearts closed night and day against evil. Only thus can we keep pure and acceptable to God. This we can do and be holy and faithful in the worst "Ephesus" that exists today, if it be our lot to abide there.

TALK THIRTY-FIVE

THE PRACTICAL SIDE OF RELIGION

The sun was slowly sinking toward the western horizon while I wended my way up the rugged hillside. As
I ascended the winding path ever higher and higher, my
horizon broadened. When at length I reached the summit and turned to gaze back over the valley, the city lay
spread out like a great picture at my feet. The winding
river, with a steamer slowly moving along on its bosom,
shimmered in the evening sunlight. The sounds from the
city were softened and blended until they rose to me
like the musical strain of far-away melodies. The low-
hanging sun glorified the drifting clouds with the hues
of the autumn mountain-side. Crimson and orange and
gold, they burned in that western expanse. I gazed upon
the scene, and its influence seemed to exalt and enrapture
my spirit. There stole into my being a sense of rest and
peace and joy that lifted me out of the monotony of
ordinary things. I sat there and drank in the beauties
of the scene until the sun sank out of sight behind the
hills and the stars began to twinkle overhead. The lights
flashed out in the city beneath. The quiet hush of the
evening seemed to settle down over me, and it seemed
good to be alive and to be there.

The mountain-top is a delightful place. There the soul
reaches heights and depths such as it reaches at no other
time. Preachers love to preach and poets love to sing
of the mountain-tops of life. How delightful are these

times in our spiritual life, and how naturally we long for these seasons! How often they are pictured up till one would suppose that they are the principal things in the Christian life! Some people have fancied that when they became Christians the mountain-top experience would be their constant portion. They may have been led to expect this from hearing preaching that exalted the emotional side of religion. It may be that when they were converted their new-born joys seemed to be unending. They thought that this exaltation of spirit was the normal state of a Christian. They gloried in it as the days passed by. The time came, however, when this emotional glow subsided. As the barometer of their feelings fell, they began to question themselves thus: "What is the matter with me? Have I done something wrong? Am I mistaken in thinking that I was saved?" Thus, their faith fell with their emotions. After a while their emotions rose again, and their faith rose with their emotions. Now they knew that they were all right.

There are times when we seem to draw near to God in prayer, when the sight and sound of the world is shut out. An inexpressible sweetness and joy and satisfaction come into the heart. How near God seems! How calm and precious is the hour! How our spirits drink in of the water of life! How we seem to talk face to face with our Lord, and how the curtain seems drawn back till our eyes behold the secrets of the Eternal! We give ourselves over to the supreme enjoyment of the hour. But alas! in a short time we find ourselves no longer on the mountain, but out in the broad plain of life, and how tame and monotonous is that plain when we think of the mountain!

In this the natural and the spiritual are alike. What would you think of the man who would build a store upon the mountain-top, apart from the throng of purchasers whose business he desired? Would you think that wisdom was displayed? Do business men do this way? No, they seek the busy street that is trodden by a multitude, where flows the constant stream of traffic; and there, amid the noise and dust and hurry, they ply their trade with little thought of the mountain-top.

The mountain-top is a very good place to which to make an excursion now and then. It is the place to spend our holidays, but it is not the place for the real accomplishments of life. When we wish to make a living, we must leave the mountain-top with its far-flung panorama of beauty. We must roll up our sleeves and take up the rugged toil and, mid sweat and grime and noise and discord, produce the real results that feed and clothe and shelter us. The real accomplishments of life are not on the mountain-top, but in the monotonous, soul-trying daily grind of business. If you imagine that you are to live in the idealism of a mountain-top experience, you will find yourself coming short of it most of the time. You will be continually lamenting over your failure to make your experience measure to your ideal. So long as you are reaching toward this ideal and are conscious of your failure to reach it, your attention will be absorbed by this, and you will be of little use to God. The sooner you come down to the place where you stop condemning yourself because your emotions are not always joyous or because you can not always pray with that full outpouring of soul, the better it will be for you. You will never become a practical Christian till you learn that the Christian life, like the natural life, is largely made up of a monotonous round of duties.

There is little of glamor or brilliancy in labor or ordinary things. That is reserved for the special things in life. It is true that there is joy in the toil and in the hardness, yea, even in the bitterness, if there is a consciousness of duty well done. It is the daily grind that tests the faithfulness. God wants people who will be true in the daily toil of life, who will do well the little, uninteresting things. He wants practical Christians, people who are willing to do the work even if it means weariness, even if it means little of emotion, even if it means sacrifice.

If you lived on the mountain-top always, the scene would soon lose its beauty, and you would soon forget its loveliness. When, after the days of toil, after the months of the prosaic, you lay aside your tools and turn from your labors, it is then that you can go out and enjoy the beauties of nature. It is then that you can enter into her moods and be her comrade. You can enjoy her then and be refreshed by her as you could not be without those weary days of toil. Many people are willing to enjoy, but they shun the work. In natural things we call such persons lazy.

Idealism has its place in life, but it must not close our eyes to the practical side of life. Enjoy what of the mountain-top God may give to you, but do not count this the ordinary, usual thing of Christian life. Learn to enjoy the toil. Learn to find the sweetness that is in it. Learn to find the beauty in the common things of life, for some of the most common things are among the most beautiful when our eyes are taught to see their beauty. The Christian life is preeminently a life of service. That is its highest and broadest purpose. To try to be a Christian merely for the joy that is to be found in it is often to render ourselves miserable. To seek happiness for ourselves as the chief end of life is a very unworthy purpose, and is one that can but end in disappointment.

See that you do your part in life in the every-day things, and God will permit you to live on the mountain as he sees best. Appreciate the mountain experiences when they come, but do not let them make you despise the common things.

TALK THIRTY-SIX

DO YOU NEED PATIENCE?

Have you not often heard people say, "My greatest need is more patience"? Possibly you feel just that way yourself. There is probably no lack that so quickly and persistently manifests itself as this lack, which can not exist without revealing itself, for in order to possess patience one must employ it in his every-day life. Many people who do not understand its real nature nor how to come into possession of it realize their need of it.

Much of the teaching on the subject of patience proves to be ineffectual because the teacher himself does not understand his subject. Sometimes it is taught that all impatience comes from sin in the heart, and that if one manifests a lack of patience he is not sanctified. Such teaching can come only from a misapprehension of the facts. Sanctification is a wonderful thing, and it does wonderful things for us. It purifies, softens, and refines our whole nature; but it does not perfect our natural faculties, and patience is one of these natural faculties, or qualities. There is an impatience, however, that has its root in sin, and which is itself sinful. The blood-cure reaches and eradicates this type. There is also a natural impatience. How much we have of this depends largely upon our general make-up. A lack of discrimination between these two kinds of impatience often causes souls great distress. Before we teach on the subject, we ought to be sure we have the distinction clearly drawn in our own minds.

Patience is a matter of temperament, of grace, and of cultivation. Some people are patient by nature. They can take almost anything patiently. Sometimes this is from natural calmness of disposition; sometimes it is the result of lack of spirit. But in any case, such a person will be more naturally patient when saved than will others who are of a different temperament. Salvation does not destroy our natural temperaments.

Grace goes far towards supplying us with patience, but grace alone will not always be sufficient; therefore patience must also be a thing of cultivation. We are told to "add patience." This means that not all our patience comes by grace, but that some of it comes by works. In our sinful lives we cultivate impatience by acting out our feelings of impatience. The more we put our feelings into action, the more impatient we become. When we are saved, we begin to act out patience, and the more we act it out, the more patient we become in our nature.

Patience is largely a matter of the proper use of the will. The Bible does not say, "Feel patient," for our feelings are largely involuntary; but it says, "Be patient," that is, *act patiently*, for our actions are voluntary. There are those who, when waiting for a train, can not sit still. Such an individual walks up and down the platform and looks at his watch again and again. He sits down and rises again, and turns this way and that way. Another sits quietly and is unperturbed. It matters not to him if he does have to wait a while. It is no task for him to be patient. He is of a patient temperament. The other is quite the opposite.

Because of this, however, we can not say that one has more salvation than the other. Both are feeling naturally. The difference is in their natures, in their temperaments, and not in their hearts.

The fact that we are exhorted again and again to be patient signifies that the acting out of patience is a matter of our wills. No matter how pure our hearts are, we have tests of patience. A pure heart is not an automatic heart, working out things independently of the will. When we have a pure heart, our will is fully set to do right, and through our will we regulate our actions so that they are right. Our feelings are *influenced* by the will, but are not *controlled* by it. We can not help feeling sad or joyous when there is an occasion that influences our feelings. So we can not but feel impatient sometimes; that is, things will try our patience, and we find that our feelings respond, in some degree at least, to those circumstances. The degree of response will depend upon our temperament, and the amount of grace we have, and how much we have cultivated patience.

Do not forget that we are not told to feel patient, but to "be patient," though we should be careful to control our feelings so far as is possible by the force of will. When an impatient feeling comes, we do one of two things: we either yield to it and act it out, or we resist it and act patiently. The latter is what we should always do. When we are full of joy and everything is going smoothly, it is easy to believe that we have plenty of patience; but in time of stress, of trial, when we are weak or suffering in body, when we are weary or feel discouraged, then it is that we most readily feel impatient. It is not that we have less patience at such times, but that impatience more easily manifests itself. We should at all times resist every feeling of impatience, yet we should not condemn ourselves for feeling what we can not help feeling. We should not think that we are not sanctified simply because we are not so patient as we desire to be.

It is natural for a saved person to long for greater patience to endure and suffer. We should do all in our power to grow in patience. "But how shall I add patience?" you may ask. There are two things to do. First, pray; and second, cultivate patience. Make it a practise day by day never to yield to an impatient feeling. Let this attitude be manifested by word and act. Reflect upon the patience of Jesus and study to know what is the Scriptural ideal. When your patience is tried, deliberately take hold of yourself by your will-power and make yourself act and speak as you know you should. By following this rule you will become more and more patient. This is the only possible way of adding patience.

We become in nature the reflection of our acts. Good acts repeated become good habits. Good habits followed out make good character. Not that good habits will save or take the place of grace, but they are equally necessary in the formation of Christian character. "Let patience have her perfect work, that ye may be perfect and entire, wanting nothing."

TALK THIRTY-SEVEN

STUMBLING-STONES, OR STEPPING-STONES?

Things may be stumbling-stones or stepping-stones to us. They may be hindrances or helps—trials or blessings. What they prove to be depends not so much on their nature as upon our attitude toward them. It is not our opportunities that count, but the use that we make of them. It is not how much money we possess, but the wisdom we display in its expenditure. It is not how many obstacles we meet in life, but the manner in which we meet them. It is not the soul who has the fewest trials and difficulties that prospers most, but the one who meets them with courage and confident trust. Some are crushed down and made to despair by the very things that stir others to renewed effort and courage.

What our trials are to us depends on what we are to them. This is well illustrated in Elijah's experience. The king and queen were his bitter enemies. He feared them and fled away and lived in hiding. He was afraid lest he should be betrayed to them. He looked to his enemies; he saw their power; he looked at himself and saw his own impotence. And so he dwelt in fear. But the time came when God spoke to him, and as he looked to God he began to see His greatness and his soul was lifted up with courage. His own weakness and the might of his enemies faded away from his gaze. He came out boldly and challenged the idolatrous party to a test of strength. Single-handed and alone, we see him alk out before the assembled multitude, superior to them all. There is no fear in his heart now. He is not in the least daunted by his adversaries. He can look them squarely in the eyes without shrinking. His heart is full of confidence. He knows whom he is trusting. Throughout the long day while the priests of Baal are calling so earnestly upon their powerless god, the prophet is the calmest man of all the many witnesses. He is looking on God's side now, and he is conscious master of the whole situation. He even grows ironical toward his enemies.

The outcome does not surprize us, for we know the God he served. He was victorious now, but let us look at him a few days later. Under a juniper-tree in the wilderness sits a man, weary and dejected. He has fled for his life, but now even his life has lost its value, and he says, "It is enough: now, O Lord, take away my life." Elijah has fallen from the summit of victory to the depths of despair. What occasioned this great change? Things did not turn out as he had expected them to. Instead of the queen being humbled by the display of God's power, she was only made harder and her anger became more fierce. And when Elijah heard her threat to kill him, he lost sight of God and saw only the anger of the queen and his own weakness and danger; so his heart was filled with fear, and he fled as does a hunted animal to the depths of the wilderness. So long as he looked to God, he was victorious over his enemies and fearless as a lion; they could not harm him. But when he looked upon the strength of his foes and his

own weakness and lost sight of God, he was overcome
with fear and fled terror-stricken.

What made the difference in his conduct? Were not
his enemies the same? Was not their wrath to be feared
as much one time as another? Was not God protecting
and keeping him all the time? Had he need to fear them
more at one time than at another? The secret of his
different behavior was his attitude toward them. When
he feared them, they were stumbling-stones to him.
When he feared them not, their enmity became the
stepping-stone by which he was raised to the lofty height
of victory.

The same principle is true in our lives. If we approach
a conflict or trial with fear and trembling and shrinking,
it will very likely prove a stumbling-stone to us; but if
we approach it with calm confidence in God and a settled
determination to overcome, we may make it a stepping-
stone upon which we may mount to higher and better
things.

Sometimes things that are at first very discouraging
to us afterwards become sources of help and encourage-
ment; not that the things themselves change, but because
we see them from a different angle. This is well illustrated by the effect of my long affliction. One of the
worst things that I had to face in the first two or three
years was the consciousness of the depressing and discouraging influence that it was having upon others, not
only upon those about me, but upon many persons here
and there, as evidenced by numerous letters showing
that the effect was wide-spread. It seemed to be a hindrance to the faith of many people. But in the last two

or three years I have received many letters telling me how greatly the writers had been encouraged and helped by my affliction. The affliction itself was the same; the change was in them; for that which was once a source of discouragement would have continued so had they continued to look at it as they had formerly done. The fact that the changed point of view, or changed attitude, changed the effect shows that it is not so much the thing itself as our attitude toward it that affects us.

It is so in regard to all things. We have need to learn the lesson that one sister learned. Speaking of the early months of my affliction, she writes, "At that time it was a hindrance to my faith; but it has ceased to be so, for I have learned not to ask why, but to have faith in God and wait and trust."

Learning to wait and trust is the secret. This gives God the opportunity to bring out that which is best. How could we know the virtue of patience if no one had a trial of his patience? If we looked only at the trial, where would be the blessing? We often must look beyond the things that first appear. We must often look at "the things which are not seen" that we may have courage to meet the things that are seen. It is when we do this that our trials become blessings; our stumbling-stones, stepping-stones.

When we face things courageously and hold to our course steadily through the storm, or when we bear opposition and trials patiently and hold fast our integrity through temptation, it is then that we mount up by means of these very things to a loftier height and a broader outlook. When we try to lift up ourselves by expending our forces upon ourselves, we make but little progress. How hard it is to keep good resolutions! How hard it is to make ourselves better or stronger by the study of abstract goodness or by wishing ourselves something else than we are! We may look to the heights above us and long to be there; we may think of the noble outlook were we there, but there is but one way to attain those heights—by the slow, laborious, and wearisome process of climbing; and the things upon which we must set our feet are the difficulties that we have overcome.

It is easy to go down toward the valley of discouragement. It takes no effort to let a thing weigh us down. We can easily let our courage and our confidence slip if we will. It is sometimes easier to go down-hill than it is to stop in our going. But in life it is the up-hill going that counts. Every time you overcome or trust clear through to victory, you have made progress upward. If you see a trial coming, do not shrink and do not fear. Do not say, "Oh, how shall I bear it!"

God designs that your trials shall help you, not hinder you. He could keep you from having them if it were wise; but he sees that you need them, yes, that you must have them, or you will never rise above your present level. Look for the good in them; count them blessings. Meet them bravely, and you will find them in truth stepping-stones, not stumbling-stones.

TALK THIRTY-EIGHT

USE WHAT YOU HAVE

Few people really are and do their best. Nature has blessed a few with great talents and abilities. These persons often become proud, self-centered, and feel themselves to be superior, and for that reason many times they fail to make the proper use of their abilities. How often are they used in a bad or foolish way, so that what might be a blessing to the world fails to be such! There are many others who realize they do not possess these natural gifts. They look upon those who have them, and envy them. They bemoan their own lack, and say, "If I only had the talents that person has," and meanwhile they sit in idleness, making no use of what they have.

"If I could preach like So-and-so, what I would accomplish for the Lord!" another says; or, "If I had the money So-and-so has, what I could accomplish for the kingdom!"

"If my circumstances were different, I might hope to do something," comes from another.

But all these are like the dreamer who says, "Tomorrow I will do great things," and yet today he does nothing.

Make the Best of Yourself

You will always be yourself. You can never be any one else. If you ever accomplish anything, it will be through those powers and abilities you now possess. It is of no use to lament that you are not as somebody else is; it is of no use to envy another's talents. You are only yourself. You might as well face that fact, and endeavor to make the best possible use of the gifts you have. They may look very small compared with those of some others, but they are all you have. Time spent in troubling yourself because you are not greater is worse than wasted. The question is, Shall I improve and make use of what I have?

Man is capable of great development. Eye, hand, strength, mind, will—in fact, the whole man may, by proper efforts, be taught and developed, and expanded until he becomes something very different from what he was at first. The blessing of God will help us much, but that will not take the place of our own determined and persevering efforts.

Have you ever attempted to develop yourself? Do not think that because your abilities now seem small they never can be greater. You were only a child once. You did not think that you never would be larger. You looked eagerly forward to the time when you would be as large as grown-up people. Each day you ate and drank and breathed and exercised—the very things that would produce the growth that you desired. You used what you had of energy and strength, and thus increased them. We ought to be as wise in spiritual things as in natural things. Paul said to Timothy, "Neglect not the gift that is in thee."

You must make use of what you have, then God will bestow more. But he can not bestow more until you use with your might what you have. You are, so to speak, the raw material of what you may be. What you will be depends on the use you make of this material. The responsibility for the final product lies with you. Develop your mind, develop your soul, develop patience, courage, faith, loyalty, justice, benevolence, endurance, cheerfulness, determination, diligence, industry, and all those other qualities that make up real Christian manhood and that are the foundation of success in life. If you lack the will to try and keep trying, you will see yourself always a failure. Decide to be your best and do your best. If you will do this by God's help, you will not fail.

Use Wisely What You Have

Israel was oppressed. The Philistines had taken the Israelites' swords and spears, in fact, swept the country bare of armor. Shamgar had not much to fight with. He had no sword nor spear, no shield, no helmet. The Philistines were coming; something must be done. There was the ox-goad, but what would that amount to against swords and spears? It was all the weapon he had. But he had something else; he had courage, determination, and faith. So he started straight for the host of enemies, and we are told that he slew "six hundred men with an ox-goad: and he also delivered Israel" (Judges 3:31). He had only an ox-goad, but he used it manfully. Had he not done so, Israel would not have been delivered.

David, when he went against Goliath, had only his home-made sling and a few stones from the brook. But he went up to battle with unshaken faith in God. He had not much to start with in the way of weapons, but he had the courage to use what he did have. And he is famous to this day as Israel's deliverer.

Samson had only a jaw-bone, but he did not stop a

moment to lament that fact. He did have the three things necessary in himself—courage, determination, and faith. And we are told that the Spirit of the Lord came mightily upon him. The result was he slew a thousand of his enemies, and put the rest to flight. Have you not as much equipment as any of these men had? But the results of their efforts were glorious. If you think you have but little to use for God, just add to it courage, determination, and faith, and go ahead. You will find that the Spirit of the Lord will make you mighty. Do not worry because you have so little to give; just be sure you give what you can. Do not worry because you seem to have so little ability, or so little time, or so little opportunity; but do not fail to use what you have. Make the best of them.

Use Your Environment

It is of no use to say, "If my surroundings were different," or "If I were in some other place, then I could do better." Possibly you could, but that is not the question. Are you doing what you can in your pres-ent environment? If you can change your environment for the better, do it. If you can not, then decide to do your best where you are.

You may dream of ideal conditions, but you will not find them in this world. Whether you succeed or fail depends less on your environment than it does on your-self. If you will be true to the best that is in you, your environment will not have the influence that you imagine it will. Favorable circumstances never take the place of soul-qualities. Develop your soul-qualities, and you

will be master of your environment. You need not let it
master you. Be your best, and do your best, in your
place. Make the best of your situation. There is a way
for you to succeed, no matter what is against you. God
will help you find that way if you are determined to
find it. Never permit yourself to spend time in lamenta-
tion over yourself or your circumstances. Keep the
following thought and determination ever before you:
"I will make the best of myself and my circumstances."
This is the true and only road to success.

TALK THIRTY-NINE

WHERE THE JOY IS

A sister wrote to me recently desiring me to tell her how she might find sweetness and joy in her trials. She seemed to have in her mind an ideal experience in which she could be joyous and calm and sweetly contented while undergoing trials, and she was struggling to attain to her ideal.

This sister is not alone in her reaching out after such an experience. People often chide and condemn them selves because they have not attained to such heights. When they suffer and are distressed in their trials, they think there is something wrong with their experience, and they become discouraged. The Bible lifts the standard just to the place where it ought to be; and if we have a higher ideal, we are sure to be constantly coming short of it.

My answer to the sister was that she was looking in the wrong place for the sweetness and joy. Jesus is our example, and we can expect trials to have the same effect upon us as they had upon him. In that dark hour of trial in Gethsemane, with the heavy weight of the cross already upon his spirit, did he say to his disciples, "Behold, how joyful I am in such awful circumstances"? Ah, no! his state was very different, and we hear him say, "My soul is exceeding sorrowful, even unto death." He was "a man of sorrows and acquainted with grief." When he hung upon the cross, he cried out in agony, "My God, my God, why hast thou forsaken me?" Do you think there was joy or sweetness in that? Such feelings had no place in his emotions that day. But there was joy connected with these trials. We read that 'for the joy that was set before him, he endured the cross' (Heb. 12:2). Here we have endurance and joy, but we do not find them together: the endurance is present; the joy is "set before him." This is the order in which such things come to us. Christ's joy came, not from his sufferings, but from the result of these sufferings. His joy is in the redeemed souls that have been saved through his sufferings.

Our own trials will of necessity mean suffering, and there can be little joy in suffering. Joy never has its direct origin in suffering; but it does often come out of suffering, or as a result of enduring suffering. The order in which it works is clearly seen in Heb. 12:11—"Now no chastening for the present seemeth to be joyous, but grievous: nevertheless *afterward* it yieldeth the peaceable fruit of righteousness." This is what you may expect—grievousness in time of trial and chastening, and afterward the reaping of joy. The Bible speaks of our being "in heaviness through manifold temptations," and also says, "We count them happy which endure." Enduring implies suffering; and suffering, of itself, can never be joyful. We might, in a figure, say that suffering is the soil in which the tree of patient endurance grows, and that joy is the ripened fruit of the tree.

There are many different kinds of trials, and they have different effects. Sometimes they are like a great storm that sweeps over the soul, when the dashing rain obscures all view of the distant landscape and its beauties, when the howling of the wind, the flashing of the lightning, and the rolling of the thunder shuts out everything else and holds our entire attention. It is only when the storm is over and the calm has come, that we can look out again upon the broad and peaceful landscape. There are other trials that remind one of a nail in one's shoe: everywhere one goes, it is present, irritating, annoying, torturing. It hinders and detracts from all the common pleasures of life.

When trials come, there is just one proper way to meet them; that is, with determination to overcome them and to keep our integrity during the time that we are suffering under them. It was the joy set before Jesus that made him strong to suffer. And so we, if we would be strong for our trials, must look beyond them to the joy that is set before us. It is what is coming out of the trials that is the source of our rejoicing. If you have endured some trial—something that took real courage and fortitude—and you look back upon it and realize that you stood true, that you did not yield nor falter, is it not a source of great joy to your soul? When you see the grace that God gave you, does it not strengthen and encourage you?

You desire the peaceful fruit of righteousness in your life; you want joy, peace, victory; but remember that these are the "afterwards" of patient endurance through the trial or chastening. You must wait for the fruit to ripen. If you try to enjoy it before it is ripe, you may find it works like eating a green persimmon—you not only will spoil the fruit, but will find some unpleasant consequences.

There are certain kinds of trials that bring forth joy quickly if they are met in the right spirit. We read that the early Christians "took joyfully the spoiling of their goods," and again that they "rejoiced that they were counted worthy" to suffer for the name of Christ. This was persecution. Often we can "rejoice and leap for joy," not because of the persecution, but because of the fact that great is our reward in heaven. The joy comes from the contemplation of that reward. We suffer the persecution; we rejoice in the reward of our patient endurance.

If we walk close to God, we shall find that in the midst of our trials, even when they are bitter, there is an undercurrent of sweet joyfulness away down in the depths of our souls. The consciousness that we are the Lord's, that he loves us, and that he is our helper will be sweet in the midst of all our woes. This may sometimes be obscured by doubts and fears for a time, but if we hide away under his wings and trust securely, the harp of joy will sound in our souls though in the tumult of emotions. We may sometimes have to listen carefully, however, to hear the soft, sweet strains of its melody.

Be patient in your trials; endure hardness as a good soldier; keep up the shield of faith; fight the good fight; and in due season your soul will sing triumphant songs of victory, and the joy-bells, pealing out their merry music, will summon God's people to rejoice with you in your Lord and Savior.

TALK FORTY
BLOWING THE CLOUDS AWAY

I had been passing through a period of sore conflict. For several days I had had gloomy and distressing feelings. I had struggled with all my might against them. I had tried to draw near the Lord and to get special help from him. It was hard to pray, and it seemed that when I prayed no answer came. Discouragement pressed in upon me. I had no idea of giving up the fight, but I knew not what to do next. It seemed that my strength was exhausted by the conflict. As I lay there meditating, it seemed that all at once a quiet voice said to me: ''Do not try to blow away the clouds with your feeble breath. If you will be content to wait, the same wind that brought them will carry them away again.''

As the voice spoke I seemed to see myself in a little ravine where I had often been, with a great mass of thick clouds overhead moving slowly along. The lesson that God would get to me illuminated my mind. I saw how foolish it would be to try to blow away those great clouds. All my blowing could not move them an inch. I might strain and struggle, and try until my strength was all gone, but the clouds would not pass away, nor would the sunshine come a moment sooner for all my efforts.

So those spiritual clouds that were hanging so low above me and wrapping me in their somber shadows could not be blown away by my feeble breath. I had nearly worn myself out by my efforts, but had gained nothing at all. I had worried myself, and it was all to no purpose. As I looked back at the beginning of that season of heaviness and darkness, I could not see anything that I had done to bring it; it had just settled down upon me without any apparent reason, just as the clouds in the heavens come over the face of the sky without relation to any act of yours or mine.

Brother, sister, have you not had such experiences in your Christian life? Have not darkness and gloom, heaviness and depression, come over your soul and you could not tell why? You began to question yourself, thinking that surely there must be something wrong. You doubted and wondered; you could not tell why you felt so. Perhaps for several days these feelings persisted. You resisted them. You prayed, you struggled. You searched yourself, but to no avail. The darkness still covered you; the heaviness still pressed you down. Possibly Satan also came with powers of accusation against your soul. You blew with all your might at the clouds, but still they lingered, and your heart was sorely troubled. By and by the clouds passed away, the sunshine came, and your heart sang again. You knew not what carried the clouds away nor what brought the sunshine; nevertheless there it was illuminating, warming, and refreshing you again.

There are many times in our lives when the clouds come through no fault of ours. Nothing that we can do will keep them from coming. No matter how close we live to God, they will sometimes come. We can not hope that our sky will always be clear, but I hope you will get the lesson that God gave me that day, years ago. The same wind that brought that cloud over you will carry it away again.

Do not waste your strength struggling against your feelings; be patient and wait. Do not accuse yourself of having done wrong or of being wrong. Do not take these gloomy feelings as evidence against yourself, any more than you would take the literal shadows of a cloudy day to prove you were not right.

If you have done wrong, God will show you just what the wrong has been, and he will also show you the way out. When the clouds come, then is the time to trust. If in your heart you mean to serve God, you know it, and he knows it. No matter how dark it may become, look up into his face and tell him that you mean to serve him no matter how things look, no matter how you feel. Our emotions are not governed by our wills—we can not feel as we please to feel; but we can be true when we will to be true, and we can wait and trust. We can not control circumstances; we can not help being affected by surrounding influences. These in a great measure rule our feelings. We can keep the citadel of our soul and not allow sin to enter.

Remember this one thing, that all your struggling is only blowing at the clouds. It is easier to struggle than to be quiet and trust, but it profits nothing. In a few days your gloomy feelings and heaviness and darkness will pass away without any effort on your part. It may be longer in passing if you struggle against it. Just trust and wait; don't try to take the wind's task; let it do its own work. Then, when the sunshine comes again, you will not be worn out, but will be fresh and vigorous for the tasks that lie before you.

TALK FORTY-ONE

HOW TO FERTILIZE LOVE

Love is the greatest thing in earth or heaven. Out of it flows most of the things that are worth while in life. Love of relatives, love of friends, and love of the brethren (1 John 3:14) make life worth living. There is no heart so empty as the heart that is without love. There is no life so joyful as the love-filled life. Love puts a song in the heart, a sparkle in the eye, a smile on the lips, and makes the whole being glad. And God's love is greater than all else. He who has God's love has a continual feast. There may be sorrow and care and suffering in the life; but if there is love, it lightens all these.

Sometimes there is not the love for the relatives that there ought to be. Sometimes there is not the love for the brethren that should characterize us. When we realize this and feel our lack, the question naturally arises, "How can my love for them be increased?" Plants can not grow without fertility; that is, the soil must contain the elements necessary to growth. If these are absent, they must be supplied, or there can be no harvest. This is equally true of love; it must be fertilized if it is to grow. Do you realize that you are lacking in love for some one? Do you manifest as much affection toward your conjugal companion as you did in days gone by?

There are very many things that may choke out love in the home. One of these is the lack of kindness. If you have grown less kind in your feelings, in your actions, and in your words, love can not thrive. Kindness is one of the best fertilizers for love. Do you show the same consideration for the feelings and tastes of your companion as you used to show? There are so many people who have two sets of tones in which to speak, and two sets of manners in which they act. They have their company manners and their family manners. When they have company, the voice is soft and pleasant, the manners are agreeable and kindly. They treat their friends with the greatest consideration; but as soon as their friends are gone, the pleasant voice changes into crossness or harshness and faultfinding, and the pleasantness of manner disappears. In how many homes is this true! The greater consideration, the greater kindness, is due the home folks. Otherwise, love can not flourish. If you wish to have love for your home folks, you must show them the consideration that is due them.

Some professors of religion are like the catbird. When it is away from its nest, it is one of the sweetest of the northern warblers, and so it is often called the northern mocking-bird; but when it is close to its nest, you will hear only a harsh, discordant note. It has no sweetness in its voice while at its nest. Some people reserve all their kindness, tenderness, and sweetness for those outside the family circle. Is it any wonder that love dies in such a home? If you realize you do not love some one enough, begin to consider his desires. Begin to show a special interest in him. Watch for opportunities to be kind to him. Try especially to be agreeable, and you will soon find that this reacts upon yourself; in a short time you will find your love increasing; and the more you follow this course, the more your love will increase.

I have been asked if we should love all saints the same. Some have even taught that if we were right in our souls we would love one of God's children as much as another. This, however, is not possible. Even Jesus loved some of his disciples more than others. There were three—James, Peter, and John—who were closer to him than the others; and of these, John was most beloved. He calls himself "that disciple whom Jesus loved." If love for the brethren depended solely on spiritual things, then, possibly we might love all the same; but it depends to a great extent on other things as well. Jesus loved John much because of John's loving nature. We love those most who seem to us most lovable. We are drawn most to those whose dispositions and characters and interests appeal most strongly to us. There are those who are saved, who, because of their faults or unlovely dispositions, repel us rather than attract us. We will not find ourselves drawn into the same close relations with them as with the others. There is danger of a twofold nature. On the one hand, we are liable to love some so much that we become partial towards them to such an extent that others will feel that we do not value them as we should. On the other hand, there is danger of looking at the unlovely qualities in another until we lose sight of the good that is in him, and grow prejudiced against him until it becomes hard to feel the proper love for him.

If we realize we do not love some of the brethren as we should, let us cease looking at the unlovely things, and look for the good things, the noble qualities. Seek out these things, keep them before the mind, overlook the faults and failings and unlovely traits. Begin to show special kindness, make it a point to speak to these brethren kindly; show an interest in them. Watch for a chance to do something helpful; go out of your way to do them favors. Possibly your own coldness has much to do with their attitude and feelings. Be as genial and sunshiny toward them as you are toward your closest friends. Some reserved natures need sunshine to open them up, just as do some flowers. Have you not seen flowers open up in the sunshine and throw their fragrance upon the breezes, and then, as a heavy cloud suddenly overspread the sky and the dark shadows fell, quickly close up? It is just that way with some natures. If we radiate sunshine, they unfold their beauties to us; but if we are cold and distant, we are permitted to see only the rough exterior. Love begets love. If we so act that love in us may grow and develop, we shall be loved in return.

Love can not survive carelessness, indifference, and neglect. These things are poison to the tender plant. We can easily kill the love in our hearts, or we can cultivate and increase it till its blossoms and fragrance are the delight of our lives. If your love is not what it ought to be, try fertilizing it with kindness, gentleness, and self-sacrifice, and take away the weeds of selfishness, carelessness, and indifference. You will find that love will grow and increase, and become sweeter and more tender with the passing days.

TALK FORTY-TWO

HOW TO OVERCOME DISAPPOINTMENT

You have been disappointed, haven't you? Of course you have, again and again. Does it hurt very much when things do not go as you have planned and hoped? Does it seem as if you "just can't stand it"? Some people can bear disappointment; they seem to have learned the secret of taking off the keen edge so that it does not hurt so much. Have you learned that secret yet? I fancy I hear some one say, "Oh! I wish I knew the secret." There is more than one part to the secret. You may learn it if you will; you may get where you can bear disappointment and keep sweet all the time.

Many people prepare themselves to be disappointed; they arrange things so that they are certain to be disappointed. They set their heart so fully upon the thing they wish to have or do, whatever it may be, that they make no provision whatever, except to carry out their plans exactly as they have devised them. They do not provide for any contingencies that may arise. Their plans fill their whole horizon. They can see nothing else; they can think of nothing else; they want it just that way and no other way. Thus they prepare themselves to suffer keen disappointment should anything happen different from what they expect. This is what puts the sting in disappointment. Always make provision in your plans for whatever may happen. Always make your promises to yourself with the proviso, "If nothing prevents." If you are going on a journey, say,

"If it does not rain, or if I am well, or if this or that does not prevent." Keep the thought in your mind that something may prevent, and do not get it too much settled as a fact that you will do what you have planned. Take into consideration that you are a servant, not the master; do not forget to put in, "If the Lord wills."

If disappointment comes, it may be necessary for us to repress our feelings of dissatisfaction. If we begin pitying ourselves and saying, "Oh, it is too bad! it is just too bad!" we shall only feel the more keenly the hurt; and the more we cultivate the habit of self-pity, the more power it exercises over us. Some people have so yielded to the power of self-pity that whole days are darkened by little trifling disappointments that they ought to throw off in a few minutes. Nine tenths of the suffering that comes from disappointment has its root in self-pity. You have better qualities in you; use them. When you are disappointed, take hold of yourself and say, "Here, you can not afford to be miserable all day because of this." Repress those feelings of self-pity, lift up your head, get your eyes on something else, begin making some new plans. Your old plans are like a broken dish and you can not use them any longer. All your fretting and brooding over them will not make them work out right. Take a new start, smile whether you feel like it or not. You have many other things to enjoy; do not let this one thing spoil them all. Refuse to think of your unpleasant feelings; resolutely shut the door against them. God will help you if you try.

Another thing to learn is to submit the will and desires

to God. When our plans fail, we must submit to circumstances, whether we want to or not. If we rebel, that will not change the circumstances, but it will change our feelings. The more we rebel, the more we shall suffer. The way to get rid of the suffering is to get rid of the rebellion. We must submit; therefore, why not do it gracefully? Many times we can not change circumstances, no matter how much we dislike them. Resentment will not hurt circumstances, but it will hurt us. We need to learn the lesson of submission without rebellion—submission to circumstances and to God.

The Lord is our Master. It is right for him to order our lives as he sees best. Sometimes it is he who changes our plans for his own purpose; and when he does this, the outcome is always better than the thing of our own choosing. If we rebel, we are rebelling against God, and right there lies the danger. If we are so determined to have our own way that we do not willingly submit to God's way, he may have to let us suffer. But when we submit and commit our ways to him, then we shall have the consolation and comfort of his Holy Spirit. If we will just learn to change a single letter in disappointment, and spell it with an "h" instead of a "d," it will help take the sting out. Try it once. This is what we have: His appointment. Now, does not that make it quite different?

TALK FORTY-THREE

THE BIG END OF TROUBLE

I once saw in a paper some verses the first lines of which were something like the following:

> "Trouble has a way of coming
> Big end first;
> And when seen at its appearing,
> Looks its very worst."

Many people are always seeing trouble. They are "troubled on every side." When they talk, it is generally to tell of their trouble. There are others who, though they have troubles, seem able to put them in the background, and say but little about them. They talk of victory, of the Lord's help, and of the joys of salvation. We all have our troubles; for man is "of few days, and full of trouble," but the greatest troubles any of us have, I think, are the ones that never come. How truly the poet has spoken in the above-quoted lines! Just as he says, trouble comes big end first and fills us with forebodings.

How easy it is to worry over the troubles that loom up in the future. "Oh, how shall we meet them!" we exclaim. "Oh, I do not see what I shall do!" and we fear and tremble before them. Nearly all the joy is excluded from some people's lives by the shadow of coming troubles; but when those troubles come upon us, we someway, somehow, pass through them. Many of them, and sometimes very threatening ones, disappear entirely before we reach them; and the others, when they do come, are usually not nearly so bad as we had thought they were going to be. We always find a way through them. Many times we are surprized at the ease with which we overcome them. One brother who had been troubled all his life was finally enabled to see that the Lord always made a way through for him, and in speaking of it he said, "Things nearly always turn out better than I think they are going to."

A young brother and I once had an experience that well illustrates how trouble works. We were going to meeting one night. There was such a heavy fog, that we could see only a few feet ahead of us. Suddenly there loomed before us what appeared to be a great giant. He came striding toward us through the fog with legs twenty feet long and body towering up out of sight. It was an awe-inspiring spectacle and at first sight startled us. There it was, coming right toward us in a most threatening manner. If we had been frightened and had run away, we might have had a great story to tell; but we continued walking on toward it, when suddenly we came face to face with one of our neighbors. He was only an ordinary-sized man, and there was nothing terrible about him; but he was carrying a lantern, which swung partly behind him, and as he walked threw that gigantic shadow forward into the fog. The giant that we saw was not the real man; it was only his shadow.

That is just the way trouble comes. The thing we see is not really the approaching trouble in its true size and shape; it is only the shadow of it that we see. Our imagination pictures it as something terrible, and we

worry and live in its shadow for days and weeks, only
to find at last that we have been scared by a shadow and
that the real trouble is only a fraction of what we supposed it would be.

When Alexander the Great was a youth, his father
had a war-horse that no one could ride. The youthful
prince made up his mind to conquer the animal. When
he tried it, he discovered that the horse was afraid of
its shadow; so he turned its head toward the sun and
soon had it conquered. Let us learn a lesson from this,
and when we become afraid of the shadows of trouble,
let us turn our faces toward the Sun of Righteousness,
thus leaving the shadows behind us. The Scripture says:
"The Lord also will be a refuge for the oppressed, a
refuge in times of trouble. And they that know thy
name will put their trust in, thee: for thou, Lord, hast
not forsaken them that seek thee" (Psa. 9:9,10).

David said: "Though an host should encamp against
me, my heart shall not fear. For in the time of trouble
he shall hide me in his pavillion: in the secret of his
tabernacle shall he hide me; he shall set me up upon a
rock. And now shall mine head be lifted up above mine
enemies round about me" (Psa. 27:3,5,6).

O troubled soul, instead of looking at your troubles,
look to Jesus. The more you look at your troubles, the
worse they will appear, the more you will be troubled,
and the less you will see of God and his help. Do you not
know that God loves you? do you not know that he sees
the trouble? do you not know that he knows the best
way to meet it, and just exactly how much grace you
will need? Instead of worrying, try trusting; you will

find it works much better. Cultivate the habit of casting your care upon Jesus. Face your troubles boldly. Assert in your soul: "The Lord will make a way. The Lord will help me through." Continue repeating it until it becomes real to you, and you will be surprized how simple trust will take you through to victory.

TALK FORTY-FOUR

SELF-MADE BARRIERS

It seems strange that any one should build barriers in his own way and lay hindrances in his own path. But that is just what many people are doing. They wish to accomplish something; they desire to do something for the Lord; but some way they find themselves always hindered. They look back upon their lives, and see that they have done very little. How many times they have desired to be as useful as others! But someway, somehow, they were not.

The greatest hindrances to our success are often found within ourselves. We build up walls between ourselves and usefulness, and then lament because we can not surmount them. We look over the wall and long to be there, while all the time we are placing new stones upon the wall and building it higher and higher.

One of the greatest of these barriers is "I can't." How many people have built up this wall before themselves! They see work to be done, they see plenty of opportunities for doing effective service, but they distrust their ability. Or sometimes they are not willing to do their duty, and they begin at once to build a barrier of "I can't" between themselves and their opportunity. Oh yes, it ought to be done, and they would like to do it, but there is that wall in the way. They would gladly do the work if they were over the wall, but it is too high, so the work must remain undone. This barrier is very easy to build, but hard to surmount. The reason it is hard to surmount is because the person is not willing to try.

No one knows what he can do until he tries. "I can't" shuts out God's help completely. It leaves no room for the operation of faith; it increases weakness. The more you say, "I can't," the weaker you will feel; and the weaker you feel, the less courage you will have to attempt anything. It is certain that we can not do anything if we do not try. It is certain that we can succeed in doing whatever God wants us to do. He has said, "My grace is sufficient"; has he spoken truly? He says, "I will help thee"; does he mean it? If he does, you will not fail if you do your part. The trouble is, you do not give him a chance to help. When the opportunity comes and the Spirit moves you to act, you draw back behind the wall of "I can't," and do nothing. Have you not had many chastisements because of doing thus? Have you not missed many blessings? has not work gone undone, and have not opportunities remained unused?

Paul had no place for this barrier in his life. He was a man who did things. He believed that God would help him in all he undertook. "I can't" had no place in his life. He said, "I can do all things through Christ, which strengtheneth me." What you need is to quit saying, "I can't," and begin believing God. Throw down this self-made barrier; quit looking at your weakness; look at God's strength. Dare to do, dare to act, and you will succeed beyond your expectations.

"I am afraid" is almost as common a barrier as "I can't." How many people shrink from duty, saying:

"I am afraid I will make a mistake. I am afraid I shall not do it right." They let this fear become a great wall before them; they pile fear upon fear; and as they look at them, their fears constantly grow greater. Soon they come to a place where these fears hedge them in till they dare not attempt anything. Do you remember the man who said, "I was afraid," and went and hid his lord's talent in the earth? Read his story in Matt. 25: 24-30. See what his lord said to him, and note the result of his conduct. Are you doing the same thing? If so, what will be the result in your case? Fear will tie your hands if you allow it; it will make you a profitless servant.

"I don't know how" is a third barrier. Have you hidden from duty behind this wall? Is this your answer to God when he tells you to do something? The Bible says that "Christ is made unto us wisdom." Again, it says, "If any man lack wisdom, let him ask of God." If God gives you a task to perform, he will give you the wisdom to do it as he wishes to have it done. Possibly you do not know how, but God knows, and if you try, understanding will be given you. If you seek wisdom from him, he will not fail to give it. If we always knew how to do things, we should not need God's help to show us; but as it is, we must often dare to undertake what he wants us to do in his wisdom and in his strength, no matter whether we can see the outcome or not. God wants us to rely on him, and to go ahead in his strength.

"I am not sure" is another barrier. It is well to know God's will definitely, but many times people want to be so very sure that God has no way of making them feel

sure. They do not take the assurance that he gives; they
want something more. Reason and good judgment tell
them to go ahead, but they build up the barrier "I am
not sure," and hide from duty behind it. We ought not to
decide hastily or rashly, but we ought to decide, and then
act upon our decision. One may cultivate the habit of indecision until his usefulness is greatly hindered, and he
is constantly tortured wondering what he ought to do.
It would be better to make a few mistakes than to let
indecision hold us back from everything.

"They will think" is still another self-made barrier.
The fear of being misunderstood or having remarks made
about them is some people's greatest hindrance. "They
will think I want to push myself ahead"; "They will
think some one else ought to do it"; they will think this,
or they will think that, and so fear of what people will say
closes the mouth and ties the hands, rendering life fruit-
less. The thing that ought to concern us is, "What will
God think if we do not do it?" It is to him we must give
account. It is his approval we should seek. If he
approves, what others think is a small matter. Are we
not willing to be misunderstood for Jesus' sake?

Let us cease to build these barriers before us. Let
us throw down what we have built. Let us decide we
will not be held back from duty by our fears. Let us go
forward in the strength that God will give. Let us trust
more in God, and be confident that he will not fail us.
Have you not read that the "man of God" was to be
thoroughly furnished unto every good work? If you
would pay more heed to getting your furnishings than

you do to your fears, you might become far more fruitful. Thus, you would be more happy here and reap a greater reward hereafter.

TALK FORTY-FIVE

HOW TO WORK GOD'S JOY-MACHINE

It was a bright, sunny morning as Brother Littlejoy walked down the street toward the railway-station. But somehow the brightness of the morning was not reflected in Brother Littlejoy's face. He seemed gloomy; his gaze rested upon the ground. As he entered the waiting-room, he saw a man with a smiling countenance, and he said to himself, "Why, there is Brother Joyful."

Brother Joyful, seeing Brother Littlejoy, hastened to him and shook hands with him warmly and said: "Good morning, Brother Littlejoy. What a fine morning this is! It seems that all nature is rejoicing in the spring sunshine. But, Brother Littlejoy, why do you look so gloomy this morning when everything else seems so bright?"

"Oh," said Brother Littlejoy, "I have so many troubles and worries and perplexities, so many trials and difficulties, that it seems I have little joy in my life. I never can understand how you are always so joyful. You always have a smile for everybody and never seem to have any of the worries and troubles that other people have. You seem to be, as Paul said, 'always rejoicing.' How I wish I were as you are! It certainly must be a happy life."

"Oh," replied Brother Joyful, "I think I have my full share of the troubles of life. You know every one must expect them. We all have plenty of them, but that is not the cause of your trouble. It is not the number of trials and perplexities people have that keep them from being joyful; for some of the most joyful people whom I know have many cares, sorrows, and troubles. There is just one thing wrong in your case, Brother Littlejoy—you have not learned how to work God's joy-machine.''

"God's joy-machine!" exclaimed Brother Littlejoy, "why, I did not even know that he had one. What do you mean by his 'joy-machine'?''

Brother Joyful laughed, and his eyes twinkled as he said, "Come over here and let me give you an object-lesson.''

So they walked over to the side of the room where two machines were standing side by side.

"You see this weighing-machine," said Brother Joyful; "I will just step upon it and get weighed.''

He stepped upon the platform of the machine, but the indicator remained at zero.

"Why, it seems it does not work this morning!''

"Of course not," answered Brother Littlejoy, "you have to drop a penny in the slot before it will act.''

Then Brother Joyful took a penny from his pocket and dropped it into the slot. The indicator immediately flew around on the dial.

"One hundred and seventy-two pounds," said Brother Joyful. "That is just what I weighed two weeks ago. Now let us try this one, and have some music.''

So saying, he took a disk from the rack and adjusted it in the machine and pressed the lever, but nothing moved; no music came forth.

"Why," said Brother Littlejoy, "it will not play until you drop a nickel into the slot."

"Oh," said Brother Joyful, "that's the way!"

He dropped a nickel into the slot, and the machine began sounding forth its melody.

Sitting down on a seat near by, they listened until the music ceased, when Brother Joyful said:

"You see I might have stood there on the platform of that weighing-machine all day and wished to have known my weight ever so much, but I should not have found it out until I had dropped a penny into the slot. We might have stood there by the music-box all day and wished to hear it play; we might have asked it ever so earnestly to play for us; but until the nickel was dropped into the slot, there could be no music. Now, God has a joy-machine, and it works on the plan of the slot-machines. You can see its picture almost anywhere in the Bible. But there is a real place where you can get the joy—real joy and there is plenty of it. This music-box will play a tune for each nickel dropped into it, and so God's joy-machine will yield you a heartful of joyful-ness every time you can get it to work, and it always works whenever you proceed right. Some people merely stand around and look at the box. They see others getting joy out of it and often try to get joy, but somehow it does not work for them. The trouble is, they do not put in the coin; in other words, they do not do what is necessary to get the machine to work. The joy is there, plenty of it, enough for everybody; there is no reason why people should be without it."

"Well," sighed Brother Littlejoy, "I would give almost anything if I knew how to get joy like you; but I suppose it is not for me."

"Right there is where you are mistaken," said Brother Joyful. "Take another lesson from those machines yonder. They are set out in plain sight, and the public, everybody who wishes, may, by dropping coins into the slots, get what the machines have to give. The more coins dropped, the better the owners are pleased. They do not want the weights, they do not want the music; these are provided for the public; and whosoever will may have his full satisfaction on certain conditions. Now, God's joy for his children is just the same—the more they have of it, the better pleased he is. The more joyful they are, the more joyful he is. You are mistaken in thinking that you are denied joy. You are not denied it any more than you are denied music from the music-box. If you know how to operate the box and are willing to pay the price, you may have plenty of music. It is equally true that if you are willing to pay the price, you can work God's joy-machine all you please."

"Well," said Brother Littlejoy, "I do wish I knew how. And what do you mean by the price of joy?"

"It is something many people have not learned yet," answered Brother Joyful; "but I will tell you the secret. I will tell you how I get God's joy-machine to operate. A specified coin is required to operate these machines, but there are many different things that will work God's machine. Sometimes one thing will do it, sometimes another, and sometimes it takes several things together. The first thing I try is obedience. Whole-hearted obedience to the Lord never fails to bring me a good supply of joy, but that is a price many people are not willing to pay. They would like to have the joy, but when it comes to obeying God and throwing their whole soul into that obedience, they draw back. Often they obey reluctantly, with more or less unwillingness in their hearts, or they want to do it just a little differently from God's way. That kind of obedience never makes the joy-machine work. There are others who are willing to obey God, provided he will do so-and-so to suit them. Such people wait a long time for their joy. So long as the heart is closed up against God's commands, you can count on God keeping a lock on the joy-machine.

"Sometimes, and very often too, we have to drop some trust into the slot. If you are doubting God and questioning whether he means what he says or whether he will keep his promises, the machine will not work. When I want a feast of joy, I make sure that I am obeying God, and then I tell him that I believe him, that I trust myself and my all completely into his hands, and that I feel perfectly safe in doing so; that I believe his eye is over me and his everlasting arms are beneath me and that he will work out everything for my good and keep me in whatever circumstances I am placed. That makes the joy-machine work. Often it brings 'joy unspeakable and full of glory.'

"Of course, there is something else that goes with obedience and trust, and that is really a part of them. It is submission. Unless our hearts say, 'Thy will be done,' the joy-bells will not ring much. If we get any joy, it will be only a sort of human enthusiasm. I say the heart must say this. It is not enough for the mouth to say it; the heart must not say it reluctantly nor hesitatingly, for the joy will not come until the heart submits unreservedly.

"Praise is another thing that makes the machine work; that is, the kind of praise that comes from the depths of the heart—the kind that comes spontaneously from a deep appreciation of God's goodness and mercy. Only those who obey God have this kind. We may shout God's praise loud enough to be heard two blocks away; but if we are not obeying him, he knows it is a pretense, and it will not work the machine. One may be ever so enthusiastic, and seem to be very happy, but if he is not obeying God, what he gets does not come out of God's joy-machine. Praise amounts to much when there is obedience back of it, but is nothing but noise when it is otherwise.

"Sometimes it is patience and long-suffering that make the machine work. Sometimes when opposition or accusation come or when railing, abuse, scorn, or similar things must be borne, the joy-machine does not work immediately. We have to put a good supply of patience into the slot, and perhaps suffer a while; but when the proper time comes, they will make the machine work all right.

"A smile or a cheery word or a bit of song, a kindly greeting, or almost any kindly act put into the slot may fill up our cup with joy when we are not expecting it. Sometimes nothing but enduring a hard trial will start the joy flowing. One may not be very joyful during the trial; for the joy generally comes at the end of the trial. Some people think that it would be pleasant if they could put their trials into the slot and make the joy-machine work, but it does not work that way. It is the endurance that makes it work, and the endurance will not make it work until it is dropped into the slot; that is, until we have endured through to the end of the trial.

"Then, I find things in my pocket-book, too, that I can drop into the slot to make the machine work. Money in the pocket-book will not make God's joy-machine work any more than it will make yonder machine play music. When people look into their pocket-books and see only money, the only joy it can make is a sort of selfish, human joy. I know of people who can see something besides money in their pocket-books. Why, just the other day Brother Sympathy looked into his pocket-book and saw a sack of flour there for the Widow Grimes. And last fall one day he looked into it and saw a whole ton of coal for old Mrs. Benson and an overcoat for Tom Jones, and a little later he found a pair of shoes for Johnnie Peters. Of course, he took them all out and delivered them to their owners. I suppose you wonder why his face shone so in meeting. It was because these things, and many more like them, kept God's joy-machine going.

"Now, Brother Littlejoy, I have told you a few of the things that will make the machine work when put into the slot, and I am sure that if you will use them, your joy-cup will not be empty much of the time."

"Well, Brother Joyful," said Brother Littlejoy, "you have surely taught me a lesson. If that is the way to get joy and if I can have it as well as anybody, I think I shall try to get my share in the future. But how am I to get rid of all my troubles and worries and heavy burdens?''

''Why,'' answered Brother Joyful, ''you are working the wrong machine; you do not get such things from the Lord.''

''What do you mean?'' asked Brother Littlejoy.

''Why, Satan has a slot-machine also, and many people are working it overtime. Some good people are working it, but they do not know they are using Satan's machine.

''Please explain yourself,'' said Brother Littlejoy; ''I do not know what you mean.''

''It is this way,'' replied Brother Joyful; ''Satan has a great machine, or I might say several different ones, and there are many different things that can be dropped into the slots to make them work. But none of the things that work God's machine will work Satan's. Now, you have, you say, trouble and gloom and such things. These come from Satan's machine. This is the way it works: You drop some unbelief into the slot, and you get darkness and fear; doubts, and you get gloom and despondency; disobedience, and you get condemnation; fear, and you get weakness; murmuring, and you get discouragement. Oh, there are many things you can get out of Satan's machine; and he is very glad to have you get them. Drop in some cross words, some fretfulness, some self-will, a little pride, a little suspicion of the brethren, a little envy, or anything of that sort, and you will get a large return from Satan.

''Now, as I said, Brother Littlejoy, you have been working the wrong machine, and if you will just think a while, you may be able to tell what you have been putting into the slot to get these things that you would like to be rid of. Perhaps it is a little disobedience or self-will or unbelief. Make a good prayerful search and find out; then stop dropping things into the devil's slot-machine, turn your attention to learning how to operate God's joy machine, and I am sure you will soon see a gratifying change.''

As Brother Littlejoy walked out of the door, he said to himself, ''I think Brother Joyful is right; I will begin working the other machine.''

TALK FORTY-SIX

BE BRAVE

Be brave. Only the brave are strong. The coward is a weakling; if he has strength, he dares not use it. We must be brave, for life is a battle. The forces of good and evil are in deadly combat. You can not avoid having a part in the conflict. You must fight whether you will to do so or not. There will be obstacles to meet no matter where your path may lie. You must overcome them or they in turn will overcome you.

Do not dream of a time in this life when all your obstacles will be overcome. There is no day so bright but the darkness follows. There is no ship that sails the sea but must meet the storms. No tree sinks its roots so deeply into the soil but its strength is tested by the gale.

Upon you will blow the piercing winds of adverse circumstances. Things will come that you can not foresee. Do not shrink before them when they appear. Lift up your head, throw back your shoulders, look them squarely in the face, and with courage born of faith meet them in the strength God will give you.

Sometimes it may seem that to endure is impossible. Your strength may fail, but when you have come to the end of yourself, God will add strength, and that added strength will mean victory. Be brave. It is only when you bravely face the foe that you can know the measure of your strength. There can be no defeat to him who will not be defeated. Circumstances may prevail against you for a time, but if you fight manfully on, the seeming defeat will end in victory.

Napoleon once fought a battle and lost. His troops were driven back. One of his marshals, who with his troops had not arrived in time for the conflict, came up during the retreat. Napoleon said to him, "We have lost the battle." "It seems so, sire," was the reply, "but there is still time to fight another." Encouraged by the words of his marshal, Napoleon rallied his troops, attacked the enemy, and won a great victory.

If defeated, never count that defeat final. Attack the foe again and keep at it till you win. Bravery is a quality of mind and soul. You may be weak in body, you may be timid and shrinking, but if you will, your soul may rise above all this and wax strong in God. Courage is the basis of your strength. It will bring strength from God. But should he give you ever so much strength, only through courage can you make use of it.

TALK FORTY-SEVEN

"BUT JESUS SENT HIM AWAY"

(Luke 8:38)

How natural it is for us to desire to be in the presence of the Master, to walk with him, to talk with him, and to behold his wondrous works! How pleasant to sit at his feet and learn of him! How often we think of those who enjoyed walking with him over the hills of Judea and wish for ourselves that glorious privilege! It is our privilege, though our natural eyes can not see him, to dwell in his presence, to commune with him, and to learn the deep things of God. In the secret closet we often seem to be very near to him, and how our souls would love to remain there, but ofttimes, like the man out of whom the devils were cast, we are not permitted to remain with the Lord; he sends us away.

When we feel ourselves apart from him, it is not always because we have wandered away, for often he finds it needful to send us away for some purpose. Even those who were privileged to be his closest companions while on earth were sent away from him from time to time on various missions. Sometimes he sent them with the message, "Go and tell." Obedience to this took them away from his presence. Their eyes no longer saw his mighty works, nor did their ears hear his gracious words. They did not have the support of his presence, but found themselves apart from the Master. So we must often go out from him with a message, and, being apart from him in a sense, we shall ofttimes find ourselves needy and seeming to go on our own strength; but we must daily bear his message to the people, and while we are bearing it, what wonder if we are lonely sometimes? Like the disciples, however, when we have spoken our message, we may go back again into his presence.

One he sent away for investigation, saying, "Go . . . show thyself to the priest." Sometimes we must go out among our enemies and be a gazing-stock for them. We must be the object of their criticism, of their scoffs, of their mockings, and all this apart from the Master. But shall we not bear all these things and rejoice in them, that when we have returned to the Master, and are sitting in the quiet and silence at his feet, holding sweet converse with him, we may know we have wrought his will and glorified his name?

Sometimes he sends us forth to perils. "Behold, I send you forth as sheep in the midst of wolves." But he also gives us the sweet assurance, "Nothing shall by any means hurt you." His messengers now, as in the days of old, must face perils; and these perils must, in a sense, be faced away from the Master's presence.

Sometimes he sends to suffering. He said of Paul, "I will show him how great things he must suffer for my name's sake." Even Christ himself was sent apart from the Father. He had to leave the glories of heaven and all that those meant, sacrifice all the honor that he had, with all his joys in the presence of the Father, and go to earth to be despised, mocked, hated, scourged, and crucified. Sometimes his spirit was heavy, and sorrow weighed him down, and at last, in the most trying hour, he felt his separation from his Father most keenly and cried out, "My God ,my God, why hast thou forsaken me?" If it was necessary for the Son of God to go apart from the Father, to be sad and lonely and heavy-hearted, and at last feel himself forsaken, should we think it a strange thing if we sometimes have a similar experience?

How sweet to be with him in the secret closet and in the meetings with his saints! How it warms our hearts and fills us with courage and hope! But for our work's sake we must go apart and endure, sacrifice and suffer. We can not always see his smiling face. But there will be a time when we shall forever be with the Lord. Until the time shall come, let us be willing to obey him, even though it takes all the courage and fortitude we have. If we find ourselves apart from him, let us not accuse ourselves of wandering away, if we are doing the work of God. Heaven will be all the sweeter because of our having been, in this sense, apart from the Master here, and we shall be the better prepared to enjoy his presence when he comes for us.

TALK FORTY-EIGHT
GETTING THE KERNEL

One afternoon a mother with her children about her knees sat cracking nuts. The older children picked out the kernels for themselves, but the mother stopped now and then to pick out some for the smaller children, who watched with eager eyes and ate the kernels with keen relish. Presently a nut fell to the floor. The smallest child picked it up; and as his mother went on cracking others, he held it up to her and in his baby language asked to have it cracked. He knew that there was something good inside of it. The shell was dry and hard. He might bite on it all he pleased, but the delicious kernel he could not get until the shell was broken.

The Scriptures are just like that nut. If we wish to enjoy their richness and sweetness, we must, so to speak, get them cracked, and thus obtain the kernel, the inner hidden meaning, which will enrich the soul. But many are content to know so little of what is really contained in the Word!

How full of meaning, how rich, how wonderful, is a single expression! One single phrase may contain enough, if you get the ''kernel'' of it, to make your soul bubble over with joy all day. A single word may give you strength to fight victoriously through a sore conflict. The trouble is, people do not take the time to get an understanding. They are too ready to think that they can not understand. Learn to take a sentence, a clause, or a word, and meditate on it. The more you think of it, the longer you consider it, the richer and fuller it will become. To illustrate my meaning I will take a text familiar to all and try to show you what I mean by getting the kernel out. "The Lord is my shepherd." I have often heard people quote this text when I knew it meant little to them. But suppose we study it a little and place emphasis on each part in turn. Every word has its "kernel" of meaning, every word is full of richness and soul-satisfaction, if we can but get it out.

"*The* Lord"—not just any Lord, for there are "lords many." It signifies one definite, particular Lord; not one of a number of equal lords, but one standing out separate and distinct from all others—the one above all others. This is the Lord who is "my shepherd." When rightly considered, this one little common word as here used contains a world of meaning. We could profitably study it for hours. There is a whole sermon in it.

"The *Lord* is my shepherd." It is not a man nor even an angel who is my shepherd; it is the *Lord*, the almighty One—he who created all things, who stretched out the heavens, who upholds all by his might; the Lord who speaks and it is done; the Lord who wills and it comes to pass; the Lord unchangeable, unfailing, glorious in strength, perfect in wisdom and understanding. Baal is not my shepherd, but he who sits upon the throne of the heavens, whose face is as the lightning and whose words are as the rolling thunders, whose love is more tender than a mother's, whose touch is as soft as the kiss of a sunbeam, whose eye is tender with pity, and whose heart is a fount of compassion—this is the Lord, my shepherd.

"The Lord *is* my shepherd." Yes, he *is*. There was no questioning with the Psalmist; it was to him a positive reality. He did not doubt it in the least. He was as sure of it as he was of his own existence. But he was not any more sure than we can be. Repeat the text over a few times with strong emphasis on the "*is*." This will help you get the kernel out of it. If you are a little doubtful, keep going over it until the "is" really means *is* to you.

"The Lord is *my* shepherd." Yes, he is *my* shepherd. It is I for whom he is caring. It is I over whom he is watching. It is I who can safely trust him. I may see him looking with favor on others, helping, blessing, and strengthening them, but he is *my* shepherd, so I may with confidence look for him to give me the same kind of treatment that he gives the other sheep. The shepherd has made promises. He is *my* shepherd; therefore I belong to him and have all claims upon him that any sheep has.

"The Lord is my *shepherd*." To others he may be a judge, austere and stern. Some see him as a tyrant, some see him as one to be feared, but he is my *shepherd*. Being my shepherd and the "good shepherd," he will care for me. He will care for my safety. He will keep me in his fold from the ravenous beasts; he will protect me. Into pastures green he will lead me. By the still water I shall rest secure. He is "my shepherd."

This brings out only to a small degree the richness of the text, but it illustrates the manner in which we should study the Scriptures if we are to get the "kernel"; but we should carefully avoid every tendency to read into any text what it does not teach. It is all right to read a chapter or a number of chapters; but you will get more soul-food by taking a little and studying it well. Study each word carefully by itself and in relation to the other words of the sentence. Follow this method of study until it becomes a habit, and it will unlock to you rich storehouses of heavenly truth. Your soul will find a feast wherever you go in the Sacred Book. There is in every scripture a "kernel." Do not be content until you get it out.

TALK FORTY-NINE

TWO SUNSETS

We stood on the brow of the hill gazing out over the valley beneath us. In the distant west the sun sank quietly and serenely toward the horizon. The purpling shadows of the hills grew longer in the valley. The clouds overhead, which scarcely seemed to move, were in broken, fluffy masses. As we gazed upon the scene, the sun as a mighty king in stately majesty and resplendent glory sank to his evening repose. The clouds caught the afterglow, looking as if a gigantic brush had swept across the sky scattering gold and orange and crimson and purple. The sun had gone, but the glory of his vanished presence still lingered in the beauty of the clouds.

At the close of another day we stood on the same hill-top. The sun was hanging low. The purpling shadows lengthened in the valley. The sun did not sink in glory tonight, but passed out of sight into a bank of dark and threatening clouds. The voices of the day were stilled. A solemn and foreboding hush seemed over all, and our spirits felt the general gloom. There was no afterglow. There was no resplendent painting of the sky. All was somber and gloomy; nature seemed to await what would come, in expectancy and awe. And as the darkness fell, we saw a gleam of lightning play across the distant cloud.

How like the sunsets of some lives were these two sunsets! In my mind, unfading while I live, are the memories of two life-sunsets. When but seven summers had passed over my head, my little sister and I were at a neighbor's two or three miles from home. In the early twilight a horseman came galloping down the road bearing the fateful news that Mother was dying. Quickly placing me behind him on the horse and taking my little sister in his arms, he galloped away through the early night.

When we arrived at home, we found the house filled with neighbors. Upon her bed lay Mother with pallid face. Through the hours of the night we watched by her bedside. About three o'clock in the morning she asked them to sing that old song "Shall We Gather at the River?" With choking voices and tear-dimmed eyes the little band of neighbors sang the song. The eyes of the sufferer gazed stedfastly above. A heavenly light beamed forth from her countenance. A smile of joy was upon her face. Presently she called the sorrowing relatives one by one and bade them a last good-by. I fell upon my knees by her bedside and sobbed out my childish grief. She turned and looked fondly down upon me and, laying her hand upon my head, said, "Charlie, be a good boy and meet me in heaven."

A little while she was quiet. Then her life's sun sank to its rest. But the afterglow of that beautiful life still shines in that community. Circumstances later took me far away; but after sixteen years, I again stood upon the scene, and over and over during my stay the neighbors told me of her beautiful Christian life. Many a time during those years when I was tempted to do evil, I would behold that scene again, and those last words of my sainted mother would ring in my ears; they stood as a bulwark between my soul and evil.

The same afternoon that the message so dreadful came to me grandmother visited a neighbor who was drawing near to his life's sunset. When she came back, she told what passed while she was there. The man was a skeptic. There was no life beyond the grave for him. There was no hope of reunion around the throne of God. Grandmother spoke to him of his approaching end and asked him if he was prepared. His answer I shall never forget. Young as I was, it struck me with terrible force. With a look of deepest melancholy on his face he said, "It is taking a leap into the dark."

A few days later he passed away, and he and mother lie there in the little country cemetery waiting till the voice of the Son of God shall call them forth. But ah, the difference between those two life-sunsets! One left the glorious hope of a Christian shining forth, tinting the sky with beauty; the other's sun sank into a dark cloud of despair, lighted only with the lurid glare of the lightning of God's wrath.

Reader, what will be your life's sunset? Will it be serene and calm and peaceful, lighted up with glory from the throne of God, or will it be dark, without a promise or ray of hope? You are fast hastening to that hour. It may be nearer than you think. If you live without God, you will die without God. Take a view of yourself now. Would you like for your life's sunset to find you as you now are? If not, what assurance have you that it will be different? Good intentions will never change it. Good desires will never change it. God only can make you ready for that hour. Unless you seek him, you too will take a "leap into the dark"; for you there will be only the "blackness of darkness forever." "If ye will hear his voice, harden not your heart."

TALK FIFTY

THE SCULPTOR'S WORK

One day years ago, as I was walking along in the suburbs of a city, I came to a large shed with wide-open doors. My attention was attracted by the sound of blows; and as I came opposite the door, I saw some workmen at the back end of the shed busily at work. Near the door on a small platform stood a large irregular piece of stone. Standing by it was a man with a large chisel in one hand and a heavy mallet in the other. As I looked he walked up to the stone and began to knock great pieces off it with chisel and mallet. I paused to watch him, my curiosity aroused to know what he was doing in his apparently aimless work.

As I watched, he continued breaking large flakes and pieces from the stone; and so far as I could see, he was just simply breaking it to pieces. I wondered what he wanted such pieces of stone for. But presently he began to kick them out of the way as if he had no use for them, and so I wondered still more what he was doing. After a time he stepped over to his work-box, took another chisel and a lighter mallet, and began to knock off more pieces of the stone. For a long time this continued. I could not tell what the outcome would be. So far I had seen nothing but destruction. From time to time he changed tools; but still he cut away pieces of stone in the same seemingly aimless fashion. At length he began to cut depressions into the stone here and there.

A long time I watched him, still wondering. At last

he made a few quick strokes on one end of the stone, and I saw the outline of a head appear. A few more strokes, and I exclaimed within myself, "A lion!" I watched until the head became more distinct and life-like. Then under the quick strokes of the biting chisel, one paw appeared, then another; and as I watched, the whole figure took outline, and I knew that what seemed to be only an aimless work of destruction was instead the skilled work of a sculptor.

I had seen only the block of stone; but within that block of stone he had seen the beautiful figure of the king of beasts. The work that seemed to me to be without purpose, now proved to have been full of purpose. The pieces of stone cut off were merely so much waste-material that hid the beautiful statue.

I knew now that what would be left of the stone after the sculptor had completed his work would go to adorn some fine building and to be looked upon and admired by many people. No one had admired it in its former state. It was only a block of stone, unattractive and of little value. But it would now be a thing of beauty to be treasured. Yet that change could take place only when the sharp steel had bitten away all useless parts.

I went away thoughtful. I realized that that was a great allegory of life. The great Sculptor sees in every human being, no matter how rough and irregular, great possibilities. Whereas we can see only the exterior, he sees within the potential image with which he would adorn his glorious building above. Man was created in the image of God, but that image is now obscured by sin and its results. And so the divine

Sculptor must do with us as the sculptor did with the stone. He must bring to bear upon us the sharp chisel of circumstances, of disappointment, of trial. It seems that these things will destroy us. It seems that these things are evil, and we shrink from them. Some think that God is not just toward them. Some cry out in pain. Some mourn and lament. Some cry to God to stay his hand. And many, oh, how many! rebel. They can not see what it means. They feel that it is all wrong. Sometimes they murmur against God and their hearts grow bitter; but all the time the Master Sculptor with his sharp chisel of pain is only trying to carve in their natures and characters his own image.

You want to be in his image, do you not? You desire the beautiful lines of righteousness, purity, truth, meekness, faithfulness, and kindness to appear in you. You want to be a part of the adornment of the heavenly temple. If you would be not a mere block of stone without form or beauty, but the image of the Creator, you must let Pain do her work in you; there is only one way. Christian character comes only through pain. If you shrink and murmur or if you rebel, that image may be marred forever.

Think not that God will let your life be ruined. He wants you for the adornment of his palace. So when pain comes—the pain of sorrow, of bereavement, of temporal loss, of being reproached and having your name cast out as evil, of being wounded by the tongue of slander—in whatever form pain comes to you, hold still; bear it patiently; it will work out in your life God's great design.

Would you have patience? You must have many
things to try your patience. Would you have meekness?
You can obtain it only through endurance. Would you
have faith? You must meet and overcome many obstacles. God puts in us latent qualities of good, but
these can be brought to view in the solid structure of
Christian character only by long and continued chisel-
ing. "Beloved, think it not strange concerning the
fiery trial which is to try you, as though some strange
thing happened unto you" (1 Pet. 4:12). "Which *is*
to try you"—did you ever notice that? It does not say
which *may* try you or which *probably* will try you; it
says, "Which *is* to try you." That signifies that it was
intended to try you. It was meant for that purpose; it
does not come by accident. Trials are necessary. If you
are ever to be what God wants you to be, you need trials,
you must have them; you can never be strong or patient
or meek or brave or possess any other virtue God wants
you to have unless you stand the test. "Many shall be purified, made white, and tried." God will do the purifying;
and he will also see that we get our "trying." "After
that ye have suffered a while," Peter says, God will
"make you perfect, stablish, strengthen, settle you."

The chisel pain must do its work. Even Jesus was
"made perfect through suffering." Let us bear it manfully, yea, joyfully, knowing that it will leave its mark
upon us, even the mark of our Lord Jesus Christ. It
will bring out the beauty and richness of the Christ-life
and fit us to be in His presence forever.

TALK FIFTY-ONE

WHEN CONSCIENCES DIFFER

Function of Conscience

Conscience is that faculty of the mind which in its normal state approves of what we believe to be right and disapproves of what we believe to be wrong. It is not its function to decide what is right and what is wrong—that belongs to the faculty of judgment. Judgment decides; then conscience enforces that decision. Conscience is therefore dependent on judgment.

How Scruples Are Formed

Conscientious scruples are formed in three ways: (1) by the acceptance and belief of what is taught by others; (2) by what we come to believe as a result of our own reasoning; and (3) by a combination of these two. The majority of people accept what they are taught, or at least what appeals to them in what is taught, and give very little thought to the matter. In fact, some people are like phonograph records, merely retaining and giving out the impressions made upon them by other minds. Often people find themselves believing things for belief of which they can give no reason. They can not tell why they believe them nor when they began to believe them. If such a belief involves morals, it regulates a person's conscience, and scruples for which the person can assign no cause is the result. Such scruples are just as binding as any others.

Why Consciences Differ

Since scruples arise, not necessarily from absolute truth, but from what people *believe* to be truth, regardless of whether it is truth or not, and since people are taught differently and also reason differently, different standards of judgment result and consciences differ. Even the best and most conscientious men have differed widely from each other. There never has been a time when all consciences were in agreement, and we need never look for such a time. Such texts as "They shall see eye to eye," "Be ye all of one mind," etc., are sometimes quoted as applying to this subject. The careful thinker, however, does not make this mistake.

Belief or judgment is the sum of our thoughts on any particular subject. Those who are acquainted with the laws of mind are aware of the fact that there is a wide difference in the way different minds handle any set of facts. One is deeply impressed by one fact, or supposed fact, while another mind is impressed very little by it but is deeply impressed by some other fact. This may lead two minds to very different conclusions. There is no way to change this; even God himself can not change it without changing the laws of mind. So long as the human mind is imperfect, so long will men differ in judgments; and so long as they differ in judgments, so long will they differ in their consciences. And so long as people are taught differently and are brought under different influences, so long will they differ in conscientious scruples. The Bible takes this for granted, and shows how to prevent disastrous clashes resulting from such a state (Romans 14 and elsewhere).

This difference was seen in the early church on the question of keeping the law. The great majority of the Jews had their consciences so bound to the law that it was impossible for them to break away from it. They could by no means understand how any one could be saved and not keep the law. Though God revealed to the apostles that the law was done away, multitudes of the Jewish Christians were never able to adjust their consciences to the changed conditions, but held to the law and were held by it in conscience to the end of their lives. The same principle is seen working through the ages. The Friends, or Quakers, because of the teaching of their founder, had the strongest of scruples against going to war; while John Wesley approved of the Methodists' joining the English army and it is said offered to raise a regiment himself. No one can question that both were equally devoted men of God and equally sincere. Others have differed just as much on such questions as slavery, holding office, wearing the head-covering for women, shaving, and a thousand other subjects.

The same teaching will not make all consciences the same, for different minds are differently impressed by the same teaching. Not only so, but past influences linger. Take one who has been brought up under strong Sabbatarian influences and another who has not. Teach them both what the Bible says on the subject, and the effect is likely to be very different.

Change of Conscience

Conscience does not readily change; it is loathe to give up what it has once held. It clings to its scruples even after the mind's opinion changes, and in consequence the person can not feel easy sometimes even though he is fully convinced that what he is doing is proper and right. This, instead of being a bad feature, is a most excellent one. It makes conscience a bulwark against evil. There is great danger in trying to force conscience. Never do what you can not do with an easy conscience. If you see that it is your privilege to do certain things and that such would not be displeasing to God, but your conscience still in some way protests against it, do not be in a hurry; do not force your conscience. If you do, it will result in loss of spirituality and in real damage to your conscience. Wait till the truth you see mentally, becomes a part of your inner consciousness and your conscience becomes sufficiently used to it not to be violated nor wounded by it. I am persuaded that some suffer spiritually for having forced their consciences to adopt something when they could not do so without a protest. Let us guard conscience; it is a precious jewel.

Effect When Consciences Differ

On any subject our own views always appear to us the best and clearest; we can not understand why any one else should view the subject in a different light from that in which we view it. It seems clear to us. The arguments for our view look so unanswerable that we can not help feeling that if the other fellow looked at it right, he would see it just as we do. It seems unexplainable that the arguments which convince us do not

convince him. Of course we are right! Do we not
see as clearly as it is possible to see?

We can not keep things from looking thus to us; but
right here we face danger. We are likely to belittle
another's reasoning and to think that he is our inferior
mentally or to think that he is not honest or that he is
a compromiser. If such feelings are given place to,
they will show themselves in our behavior. I have often
seen people do things that my conscience would not permit me to do. I could not feel easy. Seeing such a
thing, naturally tends to create suspicion and lack of
confidence. We can not but feel that our conscience is
right in the matter; and it is natural to think and feel
that if we are right those who take greater liberty are
wrong. On the other hand, if our conscience is broader
than our brother's and we can do in all good conscience
toward God what his conscience would not permit at all,
there is a tendency for us to despise him as being narrow and extreme and fanatical.

Attitude to Others

We must often meet such conditions. How shall we
meet them? My conscience is to me a standard; my
brother's conscience is to him a standard. These standards differ. What shall be done? Which standard
shall prevail? Where the Bible speaks, it of course is
always the standard, and its voice should be final; but
it is not of such things that I speak. Of things that are
properly and of necessity matters of conscience, my
conscience is my standard; but shall I attempt to make
it a universal standard? I can but feel that it ought

to be and that all my brethren ought to feel and do as
I do; but if they do not, can I feel good or retain confidence in them? And if one conscience is to be the
standard, does not my brother feel that his should be
that standard? Both can not be, for they differ.

Right here is a delicate point. I am going to suffer
and my brother is going to suffer; for he can not make
my conscience his standard nor can I make his conscience my standard. Nor can a third party make either
of our standards his standard. The fact is, my conscience is a standard for me, but for no one else; and
my brother's conscience is a standard for him only.
The moment I try to bind my conscience on another as
the law of his life, I transgress against him; and when
he tries to make his conscience the law of my life, he
wrongs me. A recognition of this fact is absolutely
necessary. If we are to maintain right relations, we
must give to our brother the same liberty to follow his
conscience as we wish in following our own, and this
without losing our confidence in him or our esteem for
him. God's work has suffered untold hurt in the past,
when the conscience of one or a number has been made
the standard for all.

There are those whose consciences will let them do almost anything. These show that they have no conscience toward God and are to be dealt with from the
standpoint of the Bible, not according to conscience.
Where consciences differ, there is need of mutual con-
cessions. I must retain confidence in my brother, and
he in me. I must keep kindly feelings toward him,
and he the same toward me. Both have need of patience

and forbearance. We must not judge each other. We must keep in view the thought that we are both sons of the one great Father and that each is responsible to him. I must not let my narrow conscience rob him of his liberty, and should not let his liberty become a stumbling-block to me. There is only one thing that can prevent friction, and that is love. Where people "love as brethren," they are ready to sacrifice for each other. Love will make our words and our feelings toward each other tender. It will help us retain confidence and sympathy and brotherly kindness, and we can live in peace and unity, even though our consciences do differ.

TALK FIFTY-TWO

THE HELPLESSNESS OF THE GOSPEL

Much has been said about the power of the gospel. It is "the power of God unto salvation." By it millions have been redeemed and cheered and comforted and inspired. Others have been warned in tones of thunder to awakened consciences. It has been the greatest civilizer known. But however great its power and influence, however wonderful its accomplishments, there are conditions under which it is pitifully helpless, under which it can do nothing to help the perishing masses. You may take your Bible into a heathen land or to a race of another language, and though all its truth, its promises and warnings, its light and glory, are within its lids, yet it is dumb. It speaks not to them. They perish all around it. They remain in darkness, when light is there, heavenly, glorious light. Not a ray reaches them. It is helpless. It is voiceless; it speaks not to them its story of love. In your own home it may lie closed and silent. Visitors come and go, but it helps them not. Your children hear not its voice. Your neighbors receive not its counsel, warnings, nor promises. How helpless it is! Oh the many dumb Bibles in our land! If they only had tongues, what messages they would speak to the people! You have a tongue. Do you not often use it in a way that is of little profit either to you or to others? The Bible has no tongue to use. Will you lend it yours? Will you let it speak its message with your tongue? Must your neighbors be lost because your Bible has no voice? O brother, sister, let your Bible be no longer dumb. Give it a tongue. There are hearts all around you needing its truth. Will you speak for it? A silent and voiceless Bible—what can be more helpless?

Again, if a tongue be lent it and its message be spoken and repeated again and again, what can it do if it is not believed? It is the power of God in this world only to "them that believe." If we will not believe it, it can do us no good. It can not save or comfort or heal unless it is believed. Will you give it a believing heart? Unless you do, it is absolutely powerless to help you. Oh, how helpless is an unbelieved Bible!

And though it have a voice and speak ever so clearly, what can it do if the ears be closed against it? If "having ears, we hear not," but close our minds and hearts against its voice, it will profit us nothing. It can help not the least. Oh, give it a listening ear and heart!

The Bible has no hands. It can not reach out to the needy nor go about doing good. It can not clothe the naked nor feed the hungry. Why not give your hands to the gospel's use, that it may not be longer helpless?

It has no feet. It can not go from place to place, but must remain supine wherever it is put. It is a poor "shut-in." Who will pity its helplessness and give it feet, that it may go to the nations?

It has no money. It is as poor as a pauper. It can not pay its way to the yearning, hungry souls that await its coming. It needs its way paid to India, to Africa, to China. It needs to go to the ends of the earth. You can send some of its messages afar for a few cents, and perchance thus help it to reach a soul ready and waiting that will otherwise be lost. There are tongues ready to speak for it; there are feet ready to run with it; but who will pay its fare? Have you money and houses and cattle and lands, and yet are not helping this helpless gospel on its mission of mercy? Must it fail to reach the people, that you may consume your means for the gratification of the flesh? Might not the money you have spent the past year needlessly, have sent the gospel to a number of lost souls?

Oh! pity the poor Bible, which has no tongue, no hands, no feet, and no money! How will it reach the lost? Give it your hands, your feet, your tongue, your pocketbook. Behold the countless throngs going down the broad way. Listen to the groans of the lost. Behold your own friends and neighbors and perhaps your own kindred on the way to hell. Can you longer let the gospel be helpless and voiceless? What would you answer the lost in the judgment were they to say to you, "You had the 'Bible, but you did not tell us its truths. You did not carry or send it to us, and so we perish"? What will you do to help the Bible to save the world? The time is short. The shades of the evening are falling around us. "The night cometh, when no man can work."

TALK FIFTY-THREE

HE CARETH FOR YOU

"Casting all your care upon him; for he careth for you" (1 Pet. 5:7). God cares for us in the sense of having a personal interest in us. We are the work of his hands, and as such he is interested in our prosperity. He watches over the development of our lives; he notes every step of progress. The one who plants a flower, waters it, cares for it, and watches the development of each tiny shoot and bud, cares more for that flower and has a deeper interest in it than has the one who merely stops for a few minutes to admire its full-blown beauty and to enjoy its fragrance. To the one it is only one plant out of many, but to the other it has a special meaning and attraction and worth, because its bloom and fragrance are the result of his labor, care, and patience. It is his plant. So it is with God. He gave us our being; he has nourished and protected us and watched us develop day by day; he is interested in us and desires our lives to bloom and send forth a fragrance of trueness and purity all around. Let us so live that he will not be disappointed in us.

He cares for us because he created us for his glory and to fill a place in his eternal kingdom. He created us, not merely that we might have an existence, but for a purpose for himself. He wants us to make a success of our lives, not simply for our own advantage, but to fill the place for which he created us for his purpose and glory. And because of this he will use every endeavor to help us succeed in our lives.

He cares for us in the sense that he loves us. "The Father himself loveth you." "I have loved thee with an everlasting love." "God so loved the world." He has a deep and abiding affection for every soul, and even when we stray away from him into the depth of sin, his heart yearns over us as a mother over her erring boy, only his love is stronger than a mother's. He sends his servants out to seek the lost, and his Spirit to plead with them. Sinner, he loves you. Though you have grieved him and have repelled his Spirit over and over again, yet his eye beams with pity, his heart is tender with love, and his arms are outstretched toward you to welcome you to his embrace.

If he thus cares for the rebellious and neglectful sinner, how much does he care for his own obedient, loving children! How tender his love! Sometimes in a dark and troublesome hour when his face seems hidden, we may feel as did the disciples when they cried out in their distress, "Carest thou not that we perish?" Ah, he did care. At once he arose and rebuked the elements and brought the disciples safely to the land. Yea, he does care. "He careth for you." His help may sometimes seem delayed, but it will come and just at the time to be most effective. In your joys and victories and seasons of refreshing he cares for you and also in the time of trial, of persecution, of heaviness and longing, and of bitterness of soul. In it all he cares, and he will bring you through when he sees the soul refined and fitted for his purpose. "He careth for you." Believe

it. Let your soul exult in it and shout it aloud. Or if
you can in your sorrow only whisper it, let your heart
still say: "He loves and he cares. I will trust him and
be content."

Again, he cares for us in the sense of taking care of
us. His care is proved in his making so beautiful a
world to be our home. The flowers, the fruits, the grains,
the grasses, the animals, the sunshine, the winds, the
rains, and all were made to minister to man's need,
comfort, and happiness. For us these exist. That we
may be fed, he causes the earth to bring forth bounti-
fully. That we may be clothed, he makes the cotton
and the flax to grow out of the soil, the wool upon the
sheep, and causes the silkworm to spin its glossy house.
That we might be warmed, he made the coal, the gas,
and the forests. That we might be protected, he made
the stone, the wood, the iron, and the clay that we might
have houses.

He cares also for our bodies, that we may have health.
He gives us pure crystal water to quench our thirst and
cool us in fever, balmy oxygen-laden air to build us up,
and countless other blessings. Above all this, he is
himself to us a Great Physician whose word heals our
suffering bodies and takes us out of the grasp of death.

He cares for us spiritually, giving us his grace to help
in every time of need—to shield in temptation, to
strengthen in trial, to make strong in adversity, courageous in danger, and valiant in conflict.

Truly, he cares for us. Let us doubt and fear no
more, but commit ourselves to him, knowing that he
will "in no wise fail" us.

TALK FIFTY-FOUR

THREE TESTS OF LOVE

"Wherefore show ye to them, and before the churches, the proof of your love" (2 Cor. 8:24). Love is capable of demonstration. Where it really exists, it will manifest itself. It need not be made known by mere assertion. We are told to love not in word or in tongue, but in deed and in truth. In these days there are many who, like some of old, show much love with their mouths while their hearts are far from God. The test of our love is not how much we talk about it, but how much we manifest it in our lives. There are three tests of love, which never fail to show exactly just how much we love. Let us consider them in order.

I How Much We Serve

We are told that Jacob loved Rachel so much that he served seven years for her, and that those years seemed to him as only a few days. The amount of our love to God is proved by our willingness to serve him. If there is in us a disposition to do only what we please to do, and if we can, to disregard any of the known will of God, it is a clear evidence that we do not love him. It matters not what we profess, if we are not willing to put obedience to God's will before everything else, it is from lack of love.

Love makes people willing-hearted. There are many things to do; there are many ways to serve; and love prompts us to serve wherever possible. If the work of

God stands first in our love, our hands will always be ready for service. I have attended many camp-meetings, where I have noticed those on whom the labor of the meeting fell. Everybody was willing to sit in the meeting and enjoy the good sermons and take all the blessings they could get; but when it came to the labor and responsibility connected with the meeting, willingness suddenly disappeared, and a greater part of the burden fell upon the ministers and a few consecrated brethren and sisters who loved God and the people enough to go to work. I have often had occasion to call for volunteers for service, and have often found that many people who can say "Amen" and "Praise the Lord," and perhaps shout in meeting, become suddenly silent when it comes to volunteering for work. The test of their love proves that love is wanting.

In a certain camp-meeting there was a young man who professed to be saved, and was saved, so far as I know. I noticed, however, that when others were busy at work in some necessary service, he was always standing back a mere onlooker. One day about the middle of the meeting this young man came to the altar, and when asked what was the trouble he said that he had backslidden. Being asked what he had done, he said that he did not know. I said to him: "I think I know your trouble. Whenever there has been a meeting, you have been ready to go and enjoy all you could of it; whenever a meal is ready, you are always ready for it; but when there is any work to be done, you are never ready. Now," I continued, "when there is need of water at the boarding-house, you take a bucket and go for it;

when there is wood needed, get an ax and use it, or
when there is anything to do in which you can help,
be ready for it and do your part.'' He took my advice,
and from that time on he seemed to be a different man.
The reason many people get so few blessings is because
they do not love enough to serve.

There are duties for all. There are opportunities
everywhere. Every one of them is a test of love. Brother,
sister, how does your love stand the test? Love will
not grumble; it will not complain; it will not shrink
from service. Do you love as fervently as you ought?

II How Much We Sacrifice

The mother who loves her child thinks no sacrifice
too great for it. Even her life will she give for it, if
need be. The man who loves his country will, if the need
should arise, count no sacrifice too great. He who loves
God as truly as the mother loves her child or the pa-
triot loves his country is willing to sacrifice for God.
Abraham proved his love by not withholding his son.
He offered him freely in obedience to God's command.
Paul loved, and as a result he counted not his life dear
to himself so that he might do the work of God. Christ
so loved the world that he sacrificed everything for our
salvation.

We say that we love this glorious gospel; we say we
desire to see it spread to the ends of the earth; but how
much do we love it compared with our love of self?
Do we love it more than self, or equal with self, or far
less than self? Many persons spend willingly and even
lavishly for self who give sparingly and reluctantly to

God. They spend more for their pleasures than they give. Some spend more for candy than they give to missions. Some spend more for gasoline for pleasure-riding than they give to all causes. In fact, some spend so much on their own selfish desires that when a need of God's work is presented they can truly say, ''I can not give much.'' They might feel disposed to give if they had anything to give, but are they willing to deny themselves of some self-gratification in order to have something to give? There is the test of love that proves its real direction—whether it runs out selfward or Godward. If we love God and souls as much as we love self, we can spend money for them just as willingly and with as little reluctance or regret to see it go as if it were being spent for ourselves. If we can not spend for God and his work more willingly than for self, it is because we do not love him more than self. If we do not get more pleasure out of giving than we do out of consuming, we may well question both the amount and quality of our love and its direction. Often the work of God must go on crutches because of lack of means while professors live in luxury.

There is no way to avoid the issue. There is plenty of money so that all the work of the church could be properly financed and no undue burden rest upon any. The fact is, there are too many whose love is wanting in that quality which draws out their hearts into the work of God until they are willing to sacrifice for it. It is true that there are many who do love and who prove it by their sacrifices. But it is just as true that there are many others who do not deny themselves and will not even from a sense of duty, to say nothing of making willing sacrifices through the prompting of love.

It is time that we heard more of the practical side of love preached from the pulpit and that people who profess salvation and at the same time manifest an indifference toward the salvation of souls and the work of the church in general should not be left to drift along in coldness and be lost at last. A sacrificing person or a sacrificing church will be spiritual if the sacrifice is prompted by love. People who are willing to serve and sacrifice rarely backslide.

III How Much We Endure

Christ proved his love by enduring the scoffs and ill-treatment of the people and the shame and suffering of the cross. By this he proved his love to be real. If our love is genuine, as was that of the saints of old, we can rejoice that we are counted worthy to suffer for His name. Paul endured all things for the elect's sake, that they might be saved. If we can not endure the little persecutions, the unkind words, the sneering smiles, the scoffs and jeers, of the unbelieving world, is it not because our love lacks fervency? The early church took joyfully the spoiling of their goods because they loved their Lord far more than they loved their goods. God's ministers in all ages have endured hardships and perils and have suffered in a thousand ways without faltering, because they loved souls as God loves them.

Sometimes people quote the text, "We know that we have passed from death unto life because we love the brethren"; but if these same brethren do something that does not please them, they are offended and grieved and are full of complaint and murmuring, and it is hard for them to be reconciled to their brethren. Is the love of such people genuine? Does it really prove that they have passed from death unto life? Many think that the preacher ought to be willing to endure almost anything for the cause (and so he should), but they do not consider that the same love in them will give them the same spirit of endurance and willingness to suffer as it gives to the minister. Love that can not endure hardness, misrepresentation, neglect, and such things, and still be sweet and strong, needs to be increased

Love makes service sweet, sacrifice easy, and meek endurance possible. Love enriches, ennobles, and blesses. It sweetens the bitter cup; it lightens the heavy load. It strengthens the faltering soul. Let us, therefore, see that we have fervent love toward God, toward each other, and toward the lost world.

TALK FIFTY-FIVE

TWO WAYS OF RISING

The human passions are like water: left unconfined, their tendency is always downward. You can carry water upward or force it upward with a pump, but in order to do so you must confine it in a vessel or a pipe. The moment it gains its liberty by breaking through the barrier, it rushes downward. So the human passions and propensities must be kept confined by the will. When they are not, they carry the whole man downward. By the power of our wills we may raise ourselves to higher altitudes, to greater heights of morality; but the moment the will weakens so that passion breaks through, the course is immediately downward. Water is raised to heights by great labor; so we reach morality only by the greatest efforts, and maintain it only by careful watchfulness and stedfast purpose.

But the sun, with its warming rays, smiles down upon the water, and the water rises in unseen vapor and floats into the atmosphere. There is no struggle and terrible compulsion and repression, but only silence, calmness, and peace. When it rises from the muddy pool, the stagnant pond, or the filthy gutter, it rises pure and clean, leaving behind the mud, the slime, the offensive odors, the noxious germs and bacteria. So when the sunshine of God's love shines upon and warms our hearts, it lifts us up from all the slime and filth of sinful habits, clean and pure, into heavenly places in Christ Jesus.

So long as the water is kept warm, it floats onward; but when it cools, it condenses and falls back again, perhaps into the same slimy pool. Likewise, so long as our hearts are kept warm by the rays of God's love shining therein, our pure moral state is easily maintained; but when we lose the warmth of that love, lower things begin to attract us and soon we fall down toward the former level. Keep your heart ever turned toward the Sun of Righteousness, cherish its soul-warming rays of love, and you will float on the atmosphere of heaven far above the things of sin.

TALK FIFTY-SIX

GETTING EVEN

"I'll get even with that fellow if it takes ten years." Thus declared a man about another who had wronged him, as his eyes flashed with passion and his teeth set firmly with resolve. In his heart he determined to do his enemy as great an injury as his enemy had done him. "Get even," I thought; "what does it mean to get even?" Then appeared before my mind's eye a view of the various classes of humanity, each person in the scale of morality where his life had placed him. I saw the Christian on God's plane of holiness and truth. Far below him stood the moral though unchristian man, and down, down, step by step, my mental eye beheld man to the lowest depth of moral degradation.

Vile and wrong deeds always degrade man to a lower state. Every evil deed, word, or thought lowers us in moral being. If some one has done evil toward us, he has lowered himself by that act; and for us to decide to "get even" by a similar act toward him is for us to decide that we will lower ourselves to his level. To "get even" means to get on the same level. It means to abase and degrade ourselves. If we "get even," we are as bad as he, and worthy that others look upon us with the same feelings with which we regard him. If you want to get even with any one, do not choose some one below you, but some one above you in moral attainments, and labor to attain to his height, instead of the other's depths. This will ennoble you, make you better, and be worthy of a reasoning being.

The principle of revenge has no part in Christianity. God refuses to let us avenge ourselves, no difference what the provocation nor how good the opportunity for vengeance. He says, "Dearly beloved, avenge not yourselves, but rather give place unto wrath: for it is written, Vengeance is mine; I will repay saith the Lord. Therefore if thine enemy hunger, feed him; if he thirst, give him drink; for in so doing thou shalt heap coals of fire on his head. Be not overcome of evil, but overcome evil with good" (Rom. 12:19-21). "Recompense to no man evil for evil" (verse 17). "See that none render evil for evil unto any man; but ever follow that which is good, both among yourselves, and to all men" (1 Thess. 5:15). When one who is a Christian so far forgets what is right that he stoops to take vengeance, he is then upon the level of the sinner who did him evil, and is himself a sinner, and is fallen from his high position to the level of sin. God forbids us to threaten to "get even" with any one. "Say not, I will do so to him as he hath done to me: I will render to the man according to his work" (Prov. 24:29).

The spirit of Christianity is to render good for evil, blessing for cursing, love for hatred. The blood of Christ will wash away the "get even" disposition from us; and until we are thus cleansed, let us not presume to call ourselves by that holy name of Him who "when he was reviled, reviled not again; when he suffered, he threatened not; but committed himself to him that judgeth righteously." Good is stronger than evil. Evil used against evil, begets more evil; but we may "overcome evil with good."

I once asked a man why he did not become a Christian. He replied that there were so many in his business who were trying to get the financial advantage of him that he could not do right, but must do the same with them or he could not "keep even."

But let us see what it really means to be "even." If a man lies about me, and to get even I lie about him, then we are even. He is a liar and I am a liar—both on the same plane. He is going to the judgment to give account for his lie and so am I for mine—even again. If he does not repent, he will go to hell for lying; and if I do not repent, I shall go, too. Yes, we may get even, but I would rather not be so. If a man beats me out of ten dollars, to get even I must watch my chance to do likewise to him. If I do not try to beat him to get even, he may have more money in his pocket than I; but if I turn the matter over for settlement to Him who said, "Vengeance is mine; I will repay," when the final account is rendered, I shall be ten dollars or more ahead.

Let us not endeavor to be "even" with our enemies by taking vengeance, but let us do right and win them to the gospel by overcoming evil with good. Let us get even by raising others up instead of lowering ourselves to their sinful level. Be a blessing to all. Set a right example.

TALK FIFTY-SEVEN

DO YOU KNOW YOURSELF?

Every one desires success, but not every one succeeds. In any line there are certain things on which success depends. Success can be built only on a properly and carefully laid foundation. Those who desire to be Christians desire to be successful in the Christian life. Those who are called to work for God desire to be successful workers. Jesus said to Martha, "One thing is needful." There is generally one basic principle on which all else must be built. If this is overlooked or neglected, partial or complete failure is certain. Many attempts are failures because of being begun at the wrong place. In mathematics we must master the rudiments before we can compute the orbits of the planets. In music we must learn tones and relations of tones before we can produce the exquisite harmonies of the master. In astronomy we must know something of our little home-planet before we can launch out into the heart-stirring immensities of space. Before we can rightly know God we must know ourselves.

The animal instinctively knows that the gnawing pain in its stomach is a hunger for food, and immediately seeks to satisfy it. But the man who does not know himself, who does not stop to consider and analyze, feels an unrest, a yearning, a hungering within his soul, and knows not why or what it is. He tries worldly pleasures; but they only partially satisfy, and at last render

the case more serious than before. He tries all the
remedies that he can find for his soul-hunger, but per-
forms no cure, simply because he has not properly diag-
nosed his case. It is only when he knows that the
cause of his unrest is soul-hunger for God and the
bread of life, that he begins to try to satisfy himself
properly. Women, and many of them professors, try
to satisfy this craving by decking themselves with gold
and gems and fine array, with the plumage of birds
and the skins of beasts. Men try to satisfy it in the
pool-room, by plunging into the muddy waters of the
political sea, or by accumulating money and by the
follies of life. As food is the only thing that properly
satisfies the hunger of the body, so God is the only
thing that satisfies the hunger of the soul. When people
come to know that this hunger is for God, they begin to
search for him if haply they may find him. The trouble is that people look at Christianity in the abstract,
as a something apart from themselves, whereas it is a
vital part of every spiritually normal man or woman.
The saying of the old philosopher, "Know thyself,"
proves his wisdom. True wisdom comes only by first
understanding ourselves so as to know our relation to
other things.

One of the things that must constantly be preached
to the sisters is proper modesty and plainness of apparel.
How often do we meet with those who once were plain
who now dress almost as the world! Why is it that
these things are put on? Because there is a longing in
the heart. They do not understand what this longing
really is nor what will satisfy it. They interpret the

unrest of soul as being a desire for these things, yet
when put on they do not satisfy.

No, sister, it is not the flowers on your hat nor the
feathers nor fine dresses, that you are really desiring.
You may think it is, but only because you can not
rightly interpret your soul-cry. No, brother, it is not
that fine team nor that other eighty acres that your
soul really desires. Both your souls are crying for
more of God. Give them a chance to get what they are
hungering for, and you will be surprized to find out
that you did not really want these other things after
all. If you find in you a desire, or what seems to be a
desire, for anything not in accord with spiritual prosperity, there is a real desire in your soul which you do
not realize. Sister, if you pass the millinery-store and
see a display of worldly hats and something seems to
say, "Just to be honest, I should like to have one of
those," your soul is hungry. Go home and feed it. Go
to your closet, fall upon your knees, and get a good
feast of the "bread from heaven" and "water of life,"
and then go back and look in that window again and
see if there is any hunger. There is not a bit, is there?
Do you not see you were mistaken? Your soul wanted
more of God, and you did not know yourself any better than to think it was a fine hat you desired.

Or you, brother, if you feel as if you wanted people
to notice you more and say nice things about you and
tell how talented you are, you are hungry. Go and give
your soul a feast of heavenly manna—not just a taste;
eat plenty, feast on it. Now come back in the crowd,
and when that man goes to praising you, it makes you

feel ashamed. You did not really know what you did want, did you?

And you who desire to be a big preacher and stir the world and be like a mighty man of war among the people. You are getting real hungry. It will take a lot to fill you up, but God has plenty, and you had better get to the table quickly. When you get full, though, you will find you do not really want to be a big preacher at all, have not the least desire to be. Why, you will feel so small, just as if you wanted to hide behind the cross where nobody would see you at all.

After we have a good, square meal on divine food, any sort of worldliness will "go against our stomachs," and we can not bear it, sight or smell.

And you there, you want to have your own way in everything, do you not? Your judgment is so good that all the brethren must accept it and act upon it or all the sweetness in your soul turns to vinegar right away. Go and eat some of the "honey out of the rock." Do not come back until you get enough. When you get filled up once, you will wake up in the night and catch yourself saying, "Not my will, but thine be done."

God is what you want. Everything else is husks. You can eat husks all you please and not get satisfied. You may get a bad case of spiritual dyspepsia or die altogether. Better find out what you really do want, and then "eat in plenty and be satisfied." Do not try fine dresses and rings and flowers and feathers and houses and lands and honors for soul-diet. "Eat ye that which is good." Get acquainted with yourself enough to know that all the real desire of your heart is for godliness, and that these longings for other things are only symptoms of your need of *more God* and that they will disappear at once when the soul is filled with the ''bread of life.''

TALK FIFTY-EIGHT

BALKERS

No man likes a balky horse. It is a nuisance. It may be fine in appearance, strong, and able to do a great amount of work, and it may pull along very well on good roads; but when a mud-hole is encountered, it is likely to stop, and absolutely refuse to budge, regardless of the efforts of the driver, just when it should get down to business.

Some people are as balky as some horses. When everything goes to please them, they are "good Christians" and often seem very zealous; but as soon as something does not go just to suit them, they draw back in the harness and refuse to pull a pound. What is the matter? They are balkers. Others do well when public sentiment is in favor of the truth; but as soon as it becomes a reproach to walk in the straight way, they can not bear the little persecution that comes, and immediately they become balkers.

I have seen others who made much noise in meeting and talked a great deal outside about their religion and their doings, but who, when it came time for them to make some sacrifice for the cause or to do some work that required consecration on their part, were ready to balk at once and throw the responsibility on others who were not balky. There are others who will work hard and sacrifice for the cause if they can direct operations; but as soon as they can not lead in the work, or if some one questions the wisdom of something they do, they are ready to throw up everything and quit and have no more to do with it, no matter how much good they might do if they were content to fill any place in which they could be useful. They are balkers. They will work only when they can have the honor of leadership. Like some balky horses, they will work only so long as they can have everything their own way.

There are many ways in which people balk. There are the ones who are always giving up their profession at every little thing; they are chronic balkers. God can never depend on them. Just when he wants something done that they might do if they were in condition for work, they have a balky spell and are of no use. Then there are the ones who can not go to meeting because the sun is too hot or because it looks a little like rain. Others balk if the wind blows a little or if they do not feel just as good as they have felt at other times. Some go along with a profession till new light comes to them, but are unwilling to walk in it. They stop attending meeting or quit professing or try to go on with a profession and not measure up. In any of these cases they are balkers.

Do not be a balker. If there is work to be done, do it. If there are sacrifices to be made, make them. If there is persecution to bear, bear it. If there are difficulties to be overcome, overcome them. If there are hard places to pull through, pull through them. If you can fill only a minor place, fill it well. If you have trials and difficulties and discouragements, pull through anyway. Do not be a balker. If you have acquired the habit already, quit it. Get down to business and pull your share. And do not try to pull independently; pull with the rest of God's people. All pull together. "If any man draw back, my soul shall have no pleasure in him."

TALK FIFTY-NINE

SPONGES AND WATERING-CANS

It was Jesus' custom to draw spiritual lessons from the things surrounding him and by some similitude impress upon his hearers a profitable truth; so we may get many valuable thoughts from the simple things of every-day life. The articles mentioned in the heading bring to my mind pictures of two classes of people.

The most noticeable feature of a sponge is its power of absorbing a liquid and retaining it within itself. If dipped in or placed in contact with a liquid, it will absorb several times its weight. Some people are like sponges. They go to meeting and drink in the truth time after time. They love it. It delights their hearts. They love the singing, the preaching, the testimonies, and the prayers. They absorb and absorb, but, like the sponge, they give out nothing. The sponge gives up what it has taken in only when it is subjected to pressure. So it is with these human sponges. While they love to listen, they have to be urged to do anything. They testify only when they feel duty-bound to do so or when they are urged by somebody else. They rarely pray in meeting. They are among the last in all such things. To go where a congregation are mostly sponges is to find a few having all to do and to find a dull, insipid meeting. Wet sponges will not burn. Neither will the fire of God burn in a congregation of sponges. A preacher may be full of fire, but he can not set sponges burning. Do you have to be urged to testify? Are you

ready to pray or do whatever you can in the meeting?
Do you love to talk to people about salvation? or do you
speak of it only when some one else starts the conversation? Do you have to be constantly urged to do your
duty? Are you a sponge?

A watering-can is different. It too will take in to
its full capacity; but, as soon as it is turned in the right
position, it freely gives out again. Streams of cooling,
refreshing water fall on the thirsty plants. The droop-
ing flowers raise again their heads to blush in beauty,
and their fragrance floats out on the balmy air once
more. A delicious coolness surrounds the place, and we
delight to be there. While the sponge represents the
selfish class, the watering-can represents the open-hearted, cheerful giver—one who is ready to pass on the
good things and who in return reaps the promise, "He
that watereth shall be watered also himself." If the
watering-can is emptied, does not the gardener fill it
again, and with fresh water? So, if we are pouring
out to others, we shall be filled anew. We shall not be
empty, but fresh and rich in our souls with the water
of life. The great Gardener fills us that we may pour
out to others, not simply that we may be filled ourselves.
It is said of Jesus that he "emptied himself" (Revised
Version.) He became poor that through his poverty
we should be made rich.

O beloved, God wants us to be "ready unto every
good work." Do not be a sponge. Do not have to be
pressed into duty. Do not live in yourself and for yourself. Be no longer content with drinking in. Begin to
pour out. Be ready to do your part in meeting, yea

everywhere. Be ready to water others. The world is indeed "thirsty ground."

A sponge, if left to itself, gives out by evaporation until it becomes hard and dry; and in such a state it is useless. Many people have drunk in the truth and delighted in it, but instead of pouring out to others, that they might be refilled, they have just given out by evaporation until they have become dry and formal and lifeless. That is the usual result with spiritual sponges. Who are those who are fat and flourishing, those who have showers of blessings? Are they the sponges? Nay, verily. "Give, and it shall be given." "It is more blessed to give [to be a watering-can] than to receive [to be a sponge]."

Now, face the question squarely. Which of these things are you? Look over the past year. Have you been ready for duty? Is your testimony always "ripe" —ready for the opportunity? Are you ready for service of any kind? If you have been a sponge, quit being one. Quit now. Get God to make something better of you. If we are not now sponges, we can soon become so by neglect of duty. The only safe way is to keep pouring out.

TALK SIXTY

THE FINAL RETROSPECT

There is a new grave in the cemetery today. An hour ago the sad-hearted mourners, with fast-falling tears, looked for the last time upon that familiar face. The light has gone out of the eye, and the sound of the voice is stilled forever. "Finis" has been written at the close of his life's story. He no longer is.

A few days ago he realized that the end was drawing nigh. Before that he had looked forward, and it seemed to him that his life might run on for years. But it was not so to be. The death-angel drew near, and he heard the sound of its coming wings. He then began to look backward, to see his life as a completed whole. He could now see life in its true light; for life does not appear the same when we look back upon it from the end as it does when our gaze is turned forward in the busy hurry of the days of health. When one is brought to the brink of the grave, life takes on a different aspect; it appears in its true perspective. We are usually so absorbed in the present that the past and the future have little place in our thoughts. Most lives are lived, not according to any plan or purpose, but according to the fleeting influence of the present moment.

Reader, you and I are on the path to the cemetery. Some day, and it may not be far off, we shall look back over our lives from the end. Day by day, often with but little thought, we are building the structure of our lives. Yesterday we laid the foundation of today, and today we lay the foundation of tomorrow. Unless we lay a good foundation and build well thereon, when we look back upon our lives at the last we shall find much to regret. The wood, hay, and stubble of selfish works and selfish purposes will be burned up in the fire that will try every man's work.

How much of the selfish element enters into most lives! The ambition, the labor, the planning, is for self. If self prospers, what else matters? If self has ease and comfort, what matters it about others? If self is pleased, is not that enough? Self seems to be the mainspring of most lives; is it so in our own? When we come to look back at the last, we shall find no pleasure in viewing our own selfishness or its fruits. We shall not desire to retain it in our memories. We shall see that whatever was done through selfish motives was time and energy lost.

When we look back, shall we see bitter words, unkind deeds, and unfaithfulness to God and man? Shall we look back upon broken promises? on friends who trusted us and were disappointed? Shall we look back upon wrongs to our fellow men and sins toward God? It seems to me that the keenest regrets that ever come to a soul on earth are the regrets that come to him who, during his last hours on earth, has to view a misspent life.

How many have said, "Oh, if I could live my life over!" Alas! that can not be. My brother, my sister, you can live this day but once. You will look back in time and eternity and see this day just as you lived it. Not only today, but every day, when it is today, holds the same momentous responsibility. Let us live today as faithful to God and man, as true, pure, just, and kind as we shall in the last day wish we had lived. Do not think that tomorrow you will live better, and be more kind and true and gentle. Today is your day; tomorrow is out of your reach.

There was one of old who looked back over his life and summed it all up in these words: "Vanity of vanities; all is vanity." He was rich and wise; he was a mighty king, and had great honors; but he lacked that good conscience that comes from a life well spent. He had not held back his heart from the enjoyment of any pleasure. He had given free rein to his desires. He had lived a life of ease and luxury. He had but to speak, and he was obeyed. But, alas! when he looked back, there was nothing in the scene to give him pleasure. It was only "vanity and vexation of spirit."

There was another man who looked back and who told us what he saw. His circumstances were very different from those of the other. He was a prisoner. In a little while the sword of the executioner would sever the frail bond of life. He knew the time was near, and these are his words: "I am now ready to be offered, and the time of my departure is at hand. I have fought a good fight, I have finished my course, I have kept the faith." His words are a shout of triumph; there is in them the exaltation of final victory. There is no tinge of regret, there is no tear of sorrow. What mattered it if his way had been rugged and thorny? What mattered the thousand perils that had threatened him on every side? What mattered the shipwrecks, the scourg-

ings, the stoning, the opposition of false brethren and of
the heathen, the dungeons, the cold, the weariness, the
sorrows? He looked back over them all; and his soul,
glowing with joy, burst out in language of supreme satisfaction: "I have fought a good fight."

Not once had he laid down his weapons. Not once had
he faltered. Not for a day had he ceased to be true to
his Lord. Therefore he could say, "I have kept the
faith." Though many times he might have avoided
trouble had he kept back the message of truth, yet how
glad he was that in every instance he had been true!

Sometimes you will not find it easy to do right, sometimes you will have to sacrifice and endure, sometimes
you will be reproached and mocked; but when you take
that last retrospective view, the fact that you have been
true will cause you to be glad, as was Paul of old. Then,
be true today. Fill today with a full measure of faithful service. Think not of tomorrow, but do the right,
in each today, and thus you may exclaim with Paul,
"Henceforth there is laid up for me a crown of righteousness, which the Lord, the righteous judge, shall give
me at that day" (2 Tim. 4:8).